Woman of Fire

Empower Yourself to See God's Glory

Veronica Abisay

Cover Design: Casting Crowns Media, LLC

Interior Design: B.O.Y. Enterprises, Inc.

ISBN: 978-1-7338051-4-8

Printed in the United States.

Table of Contents

Get *ready to have a* **key** *that will open the door of your destiny and be able to have more power and more anointing upon your life and all of your surroundings in Jesus name.*

INTRODUCTION

Today, I am introducing you to the POWER of the Holy Spirit because we can't become Christ-like on our own. We must let the Holy Spirit establish godly behavior in us. Romans 8:11 says, "But if the Spirit of Him who raised Jesus from the dead lives in you, He who raised Christ from the dead will also give life to your mortal bodies through His Spirit that lives in you."

Think about this! The power of resurrection is on the inside of you. We need to learn comprehensively how to tap into that power to continue running our race and keep fighting the good fight of faith. And by this sufficient grace, we are able to hear God's voice and follow His instructions. That's why the bible says, "my sheep hear my voice, and I know them, and they follow my commands John 10:27.

So, by reading this book, you will be able to understand the true power of the Holy Spirit. Who is the Holy Spirit, what does the Holy Spirit do and why do we need Him? This manual will give you a guide in understanding all of these and put you on the right track with God.

When I speak about the power of the Holy Spirit, many people, especially Christians misunderstand the meaning of the power and they tend to define the power of the Holy Spirit literally as the world defines it. But I am here to tell you from the biblical view and inspire you with my own experience as you continue to read this book.

I dedicated my time to learn about this power and allowed the Holy Spirit to teach me and take me deeper inside the spiritual realm so I can be able to know Him better. "Because when you know Him better, you will enjoy the privileges of being in His presence." This power is real and I'm so glad to share this knowledge with you.

This book will educate, inspire and motivate you to seek the power of the Holy Spirit like never before and if you're not filled yet, you can receive the power of the Holy Spirit as you surrender totally and ask Him to lead your life.

Now say this prayer:

Father, I surrender the full control of my life to You. I pray for your grace to fill me up to overflow with your Spirit, just as You have promised to do if I ask according to Your will. I ask this in the name of Jesus and believe that you are pouring out your Spirit upon me right now.

Did you know that God's Holy Spirit is as close as your breath? You can decide to have Him now! Yes, you can! Listen, knowing the Holy Spirit and being filled with the power of the Holy Spirit are two different things. Many people believe in this power of the Holy Spirit, but it takes an extra mile, an extra effort and an extra care to receive Him truthfully and to keep Him with you always.

Chapter 1

My own experience with the Holy Spirit

I'd like to share my experience and personal encounter with the Holy Spirit with you. Because, I believe it will inspire you and transform the way you think and give you a new dimension of view about the power of the Holy Spirit.

It all began when I was driving back home after long hours at church (mid-night prayer). I remember I got into my car, turned on my gospel station and they were playing a series of worship songs. I began to sing as I was driving while heading home. I still remember the songs I sang on that day, the tears and my heart's cry to the Lord that night. Then, I noticed I was speaking words that I had never used before. My tongue changed and I was driven into the spirit with the capacity of speaking various languages. I started to pray in different languages. I couldn't stop myself, I tried but I could not. I cried like a kid who had just saw her parents after being away for a very longtime.

A few minutes later, while I was still praying, something whispered in my ear and told me to record the prayer on my phone and send to my sister. I obeyed the voice and did that right away because I knew it was the voice of the Holy Spirit.

The reason is because my sister has a gift of tongues interpretation and really the Holy Spirit wanted to reveal to me what He was praying for. I later realized why He told me to do that. He had given me so many instructions and prophecies that He wanted me to act on accordingly and also to follow the instructions.

The prayer lasted for 3 hours and all along I only prayed in tongues. After I finished with the prayers, my body was so tired but my Spirit was filled with great joy, strength, power and anointing. The only thing I could see at that moment was Jesus looking straight at me and stretching forth His hand toward me and saying "It is well. I have made you a new person. You will walk with me, your moves are mine, and your steps are my steps. My eye will be upon you all the days of your life. I have chosen you and my grace will be sufficient for you. I love you."

There's no place you can hide that my eyes cannot see you nor my hands too short to reach out to you. And He led me to these scriptures:

- Psalm 139:7- Where can I go from your Spirit? Where can I flee from your presence?
- Jeremiah 23:24- Who can hide in secret places so that I cannot see them? declares the LORD "Do not I fill heaven and earth.? declare the LORD.

- John 15:16- You did not choose me, but I you and appointed you so that you might go and bear fruits, fruits that will last and so whatever you ask in my name the Father will give you.

Never in my life had I felt that wonderful! Even though I was already a born-again Christian, speaking in tongues here and there, and attending the Bible study, it was an entirely new feeling which I gladly welcomed. I was, as I like to call it, a "simple and uncomplicated believer." But I never had a face to face encounter with the power of the Holy Spirit. After a week, I started to see spiritual breakthrough taking place in my life, accompanied by financial breakthrough, and doors of opportunities. I still remember the passion for Jesus that resulted to that experience. The Holy Spirit has been my friend and close comfort ever since then.

This Holy Ghost encounter was a life-changing experience to me, and it was everything I needed to take me to where I am today. I didn't know such feelings of power and anointing were possible and made available to me. Hallelujah, Thank you Jesus!

Look! Even though I was a born-again Christian, went to church every Sunday and attended bible study on Wednesdays, yet I was missing something very important which was "Being filled full with the Power of the Holy spirit."

Today, there are many Christians that live their entire lives thinking they have the Holy Spirit, without being aware they haven't truly received Him in fullness and power. John 1:26; John the Baptist told the

Pharisees, "I baptized with water, but there standeth one among you, whom he know not." Those religious leaders saw Jesus in the flesh, and they heard him speak. But they had no understanding of who he was. They didn't know about his power and glory.

I dare to say that I was not filled with the power of the Holy Spirit because the flesh ruled over me, and I was quick to react in anger. But now, every hostile emotion had been drained out of me, and a spigot of God's love has been turned on inside me, filling me up, and overflowing out of me. I say again, for the first time in my life I could honestly say I was at peace and felt like a GIANT on top of the world.

Since that day, I became so in love with the Holy Spirit and I'm always trying my best to give Him a chance to lead me in whatever direction He desires. One thing you need to know is this, the Holy Spirit speaks and when He speaks other speakers become noisemakers. John 16:13 says, "But when He, The Spirit of truth, comes, He will guide you into all the truth; for He will not speak on His own initiatives, But whatever He hears, He will speak; and He will disclose to you what is to come."

Also, Hebrews 3:7-11 "Therefore, just as the Holy Spirit say," TODAY IF YOU HEAR HIS VOICE,

And Ezekiel 2:2" As He spoke to me the Spirit enter me and set me on my feet; and I heard Him speaking to me.

The Holy Spirit has changed my life and my way of praying completely. He taught me three things;

1. How to PRAY

2. How to ASK and

3. How to APPROACH Him.

The Bible says; Romans 8:26-27 "In the same way, the Spirit helps us in our weakness. We do not know what we ought to pray for, but the Spirit himself intercedes for us through". There are so many ways the Holy Spirit helps us to pray. The Holy Spirit brings to us the Spirit of the Father. Since the Holy Spirit has the same spirit as the Father and resides in us, He will convey to us that Spirit, which will help us in prayer.

I don't know about you but sometimes I just don't know how to pray. Sometimes, I don't know what the will of the Lord is in a situation and what the outcome could be. Oftentimes, my natural wisdom doesn't get the job done and will need help in difficult situations.

Thank God the Holy Spirit is our Helper. Jesus told His disciples that it was good for them that He went away because He won't be able to send the Comforter, the Holy Spirit, until He has ascended to the right hand of God (John 16:7).

"Holy Spirit"
The BEST gift ever that Jesus gave us.
John 14:16- "And I will ask the Father, and he will give you another
advocate, who will never leave you"

Ask God to give you a personal encounter with the Holy Spirit. I
guarantee, your LIFE will never stay the same.

Woman of Fire

My Daily Prayer routine.

I'm going to share with you my daily bible and prayer routine. Perhaps, you will use it as a guide to create your own or you can equally use the same guide as mine.

But this simple routine has truly helped me to be not only efficient with my time but more effective as well. I handle my tasks appropriately. I know when I sit down to pray, meet with God, and I look forward to this time because I know what to expect.

I want to challenge you today to make every effort to establish a daily bible and prayer routine that will make your relationship with God to become very strong so that you will always dwell in His presence. Because I believe matured Christians make every effort to know God and build on their faith and relationship with Him.

Here is my prayer routine;

1. Read the scripture

I read the Bible when I wake up (before I start my day) and I make sure I get time to meditate on the scripture. I have a plan that I follow every day that keeps me focused and motivated.

Since I started doing this, my eyes have been opened (even more) to the importance of pursuing knowledge, insight and wisdom in the word of God.

Jeremiah 4:22 says, "For my people are foolish; they know me not, they are stupid children; they have no understanding. They are wise in doing evil! But how to do good they know not."

Listen people of God, there is a great danger in neglecting God's word for long periods of time. We must fight everyday to create time for the word of God. Download the app that enables the sending of the daily scripture to your phone everyday or set a reminder. Because we must grow in the knowledge of God so that we might through His word gain insight and live a life of wisdom. The bible makes it clear that we can grow in our faith and holiness by reading the word of God. In fact, growing closer to the Lord should be the most important thing in your life. It's more important than reaching your dreams or even fulfilling your calling. Everything you do in life flows from everything you are in Christ.

Hebrew 6:3; Apostle Paul tells us to establish those foundational teachings about Christ and continue from there to grow to maturity. Therefore, let us move beyond the elementary teachings about Christ and the Holy Spirit and be taken forward to maturity.

2. Praise and worship

While meditating on the word, think deeply about what God had said to me in His word. I will turn on some worship music to prepare my mind and heart for prayer. I always choose music that turns my mind to Christ and invite the Holy Spirit to take over. The aim here is to turn away from myself, my worries and troubles, and to tell God that I am here to worship and exalt Him.

John 4:23 But the hour is coming and now is, when the true worshipers shall worship the Father in spirit and truth, for the Father in spirit and truth, for the seeks such to worship Him.

Hebrews 4:12 says, For the word of god is alive and active and sharper than any double-edged sword, it penetrates even to dividing soul and spirit, joints and narrow.

Deuteronomy 6:4 "You shall love the Lord your God with all your heart and with all your soul and with your might."

3. Prayer

My time with the Lord in prayer is very important and sacred because I know prayer carries power and changes lives, and also it's a privilege for me to talk to my Father (God).

- Jeremiah 33:3; Call to me and I will answer you". We have a promise that He hears us.
- Jeremiah 29:12, You will call on me and come and pray to me, and I will listen to you.

First, I pray for the Holy Spirit to illuminate the scripture as I read and also ask Him to give me insight into His word. Then, pray with my to-do-list. I also pray for my spouse, kids, family, friends, neighbors, co-workers, relatives, church members and all the saints around the world for God's mercy and love to be bestowed on them.

Afterwards, I pray in tongues for at least the last 15 minutes. This helps to keep me in tune with the Holy Spirit, build me up spiritually and helps me to live a spirit-led life to my fulfilment.

- 1 Corinthians 14:15- So what shall I do? I will pray with my spirit, But I will also pray with my mind; I will sing with my spirit, but I will also sing with my mind.
- 1 Corinthians 14:2- For anyone who speaks in tongue does not speak to people but God. Indeed, no one understands them, they utter mysteries by the spirit.
- Act 2:4- All of them were filled with the Holy Spirit and began to speak in other tongue as the Spirit enabled them.
- Roman 8:26- In the same way, Spirit helps us in our weakness. we do not know what we ought to pray for, but the spirit himself intercedes for us through wordless groans.

"Praying in Tongues is a weapon against the works of the enemy."

"I believe the best way to be consistent in spending regular time with God is to create a daily bible reading & prayer routine."

What is the power of the Holy Spirit?

The power of the Holy Spirit is the power of God. The Spirit is the third person of the trinity and as such has appeared throughout the Scripture as a being through and by whom great works of power are made manifest to us.

Yes, there's only one God. But that one God comprises of three persons; Father, Son and Spirit. His power was first seen in the act of creation, for it was by His power world came into being.

Genesis 1:1–2 -In the beginning God created the heavens and the earth. Now the earth was formless and empty, darkness was over the surface of the deep, and the Spirit of God was hovering over the waters.

Job 26:13 -The Holy Spirit also empowered men in the Old Testament to bring about God's will. He also empowers us today to be witnesses of God's love and live the life that pleases him.

This power descended upon the believers on the Pentecostal day. It was a powerful event that led to the believers to speak different languages and still understood themselves. The bible further explains the event in the book of Acts.

Acts 2:15 -These people are not drunk, as you suppose. It's only nine in the morning.

The bible says, they were all together in one place and suddenly a sound like the blowing of violet wind came from Heaven and filled the whole house where they were sitting and all of them were filled with the Holy Spirit and began to speak in other tongues as the Spirit enabled them.

The Holy Spirit uses His power to break us so that He might remake us. This procedure keeps us strongly in God's presence. Jesus promised us the Spirit as a permanent guide, teacher, seal of salvation, and comforter for believers (John 14:16-18). He also promised that the Holy Spirit's power would help His followers to spread the message of the gospel around the world:

Acts 1:8 "But you will receive power when the Holy Spirit comes on you; and you will be my witnesses in Jerusalem, and in all Judea and Samaria, and to the ends of the earth"

Woman of Fire

The salvation of souls is a supernatural work only made possible by the Holy Spirit's power that reigns in the world today.

Who is the Holy Spirit?

The Bible talks about the identity of the Holy Spirit? Simply, the Bible declares that the Holy Spirit is God. The Bible also tells us that the Holy Spirit is a divine person, a being with a mind, emotions, and a free will. The fact that the Holy Spirit is God is clearly seen in different parts of the Scriptures including Acts 5:3-4. In this verse, Peter confronts Ananias as to why he lied to the Holy Spirit and tells him that he had "not lied to men but to God."

It is a clear declaration that lying to the Holy Spirit is a grave sin and it also implies lying to God. We can also know that the Holy Spirit is God because He possesses the same characteristics with God. For example, His omnipresence is seen in Psalm 139:7-8, "Where can I go from your Spirit? Where can I flee from your presence? If I go up to the heavens, you are there; if I make my bed in the depths, you are there."

Then, in 1 Corinthians 2:10-11, we see the characteristic of omniscience in the Holy Spirit. "But God has revealed it to us by his Spirit. The Spirit searches all things, even the deep things of God. For who among men knows the thoughts of a man except the man's spirit within him? In the same way no one knows the thoughts of God except the Spirit of God."

You can now see that the Holy Spirit is indeed a divine person because He possesses a mind, emotions, and a free will. The Holy Spirit thinks and knows (1 Corinthians 2:10). The Holy Spirit can be grieved (Ephesians 4:30). The Spirit intercedes for us (Romans 8:26-27).

He makes decisions according to His will (1 Corinthians 12:7-11). The Holy Spirit can truly function as the Comforter and Counselor that Jesus promised He would be (John 14:16, 26, 15:26).

Woman of Fire

"The Holy Spirit is a real person who came to reside within Jesus Christ's true followers."

What does the Holy Spirit do?

1) The Holy Spirit does many things in the lives of believers. He serves as the believers' Helper and is always available when we need Him.

(John 14:26). He dwells in believers and seals them until the day of redemption—this indicates that the Holy Spirit's presence in the believer is irreversible and He is their refuge. He guards and guarantees the salvation of the ones He dwells in (Ephesians 1:13; 4:30).

2) The Holy Spirit regenerates and renews the believer (Titus 3:5). At the moment of salvation, the Spirit baptizes the believer into the body of Christ (Romans 6:3). Believers receive the new birth by the power of the Spirit (John 3:5–8).

The Spirit comforts believers with fellowship and joy as they go through this hostile world. He also directs them in all their endeavors to bring them to an expected end.

(1 Thessalonians 1:6; 2 Corinthians 13:14). The Spirit, in His mighty power, fills believers with "all joy and peace" as they trust the Lord, causing believers to "overflow with hope" (Romans 15:13).

3) Sanctification is another work of the Holy Spirit in the life of a believer. The Spirit sets Himself against the desires of the flesh and leads the believer into righteousness (Galatians 5:16–18). The works of the flesh become less evident, and the fruit of the Spirit becomes more evident (Galatians 5:19-26). Believers are COMMANDED to "be filled with the Spirit" (Ephesians 5:18), which means they are to submit themselves totally to the Spirit's full control.

4) The Holy Spirit is a gift-giver. "There are different kinds of gifts, but the same Spirit distributes them" (1 Corinthians 12:4-11). The spiritual gifts that believers possess are given by the Holy Spirit as He determines in His wisdom.

5) The Holy Spirit does work among unbelievers. Jesus promised that He would send the Holy Spirit to "convict the world concerning sin, righteousness and judgment."

John 16:8, The Spirit testifies of Christ (John 15:26). Currently, the Holy Spirit is also restraining sin and combating "the secret power of lawlessness" in the world. This action keeps the rise of the Antichrist at bay (2 Thessalonians 2:6–10).

6) The Holy Spirit give believers the wisdom by which we can understand God vividly and obey His commands. "The Spirit searches everything, even the depths of God. For who knows the thoughts we bear inside except for the spirit of that person which is in him? So also,

no one comprehends the thoughts of God except the Spirit of God" (1 Corinthians 2:10–11).

Since we have been given the amazing gift of God's Spirit inside ourselves, we can comprehend God's thought as revealed in the Scripture. The Spirit helps us to understand this so as to achieve our purpose. This is wisdom from God, rather than wisdom from man. No amount of human knowledge can ever replace the Holy Spirit's teaching (1 Corinthians 2:12–13).

7) The Holy Spirit will help us recall the things we've learned about God and His divine love (John 14:16), which also means the spirit will help us when we share our faith with others.

8) The Holy Spirit assists believers in prayer (Jude 1:20) and "intercedes for God's people in accordance with the will of God" (Romans 8:26–27).

You can read about the Holy Spirit and His assurances from these passages: John 14, John 16, Romans 8, and Galatians 5:16-26. But keep in mind that the Holy Spirit cannot do all the work for us, we need to decide within us to stand up to it. We are responsible to do our part like reading our bible, pray for ourselves and others and so on. Another important thing to remember is that the Holy Spirit doesn't mix with activities that will go contrary to the word of God. I have seen people sometimes justify their actions by saying "My conscience told me." We need to make sure we listen to that little, still voice of the Holy Spirit, and not the voice of our own desires.

"You want to be empowered with the Holy Spirit before you empower others. This is very IMPORTANT. The Holy Spirit cannot do all of the work for us.

Woman of Fire

What is Spiritual Growth?

Spiritual growth is:

1. Increasing in your knowledge and understanding in God's Word.
2. Decreasing in your frequency and severity of sin.
3. Increasing in your faith and trust in God.

1 Corinthians 11:1, Paul says, "Follow my example, as I follow the example of Christ." Jesus Christ is the ultimate example of what it truly means to be spiritual. So, in order for spiritual growth to occur, you first need to make sure you possess a true spiritual life through faith in the Lord Jesus Christ.

When you believe in Jesus Christ, the Holy Spirit lives inside of you (John 14:16-17) and you are a new creation in Christ!

2 Corinthians 5:17 says, "Therefore, if anyone is in Christ, he is a new creation; the old has gone, the new has come!" Your old nature, which is dominated by sin, is replaced with a new nature that is under the influence of God's Spirit (Romans 6-7).

Spiritual growth can only occur in a person who has put all of his or her trust in the Lord Jesus Christ as his or her Savior. So as a believer, increasing your spirituality is important to becoming an all-around better person. Remember, it's not about being a good person. It's about being like Jesus and following His footsteps on how He lived a fulfilled life on earth.

Spiritual growth = Spiritual awareness, which is the process of becoming more and more like Jesus.

Chapter 2

What do you want?

Obviously, there's no specific answer to this, but I want you to flow with me as God commanded me to share this knowledge with you. What you and I need is the power of the Holy Spirit to get all what we desire. God is getting ready to raise an army of women for His glory on earth. The women who will be able to hear God's voice and be ready to do accordingly to what He is telling them to do in order for Him to use them appropriately in the right direction.

Act 1:8 says" But you will receive power when the Holy Spirit has come upon you, and you will be my witnesses in Jerusalem and in all Judea and Samaria, and to the end of the earth. Now you see where am going. Right?

We have to have the POWER of the Holy Spirit to be on fire for Jesus and to function on right path with Him. Let me take you to the scripture to further stress my point.

Acts 1:5; John 14:26; 16:7 says, Before Jesus ascended to heaven, He told His disciples that He would send one who would teach and guide all those who believe in Him. Jesus' promise was fulfilled less than two weeks later when the Holy Spirit came in power on the believers at Pentecost (Acts 2).

 Now, when a person believes in Christ, the Holy Spirit immediately becomes a permanent part of his life and dwells in him (Romans 8:14; 1 Corinthians 12:13). But remember, it is important to note that we have the choice to choose whether or not to accept the Holy Spirit's guidance. It's the gift of free will.

Acts 7:51; 1 Thessalonians 5:19 says, When we know the will of God but do not follow it, we are resisting the Spirit's work in our lives and a desire to follow our own way grieves Him. (Ephesians 4:30) The Spirit will never lead us into sin.

Now you know that as a believer we have the power of the Holy Spirit right inside us. However, that power will not work until we put it to work! The Holy Spirit is a gentleman, and as such He'll not force you to turn off the television, "Now you listen to me!"

God gave us the Holy Spirit to help us do the will of God, strengthen us and counsel us. But He won't do anything until He is asked which is dependent on us. That's why James 5:13 says if you're in trouble or afflicted, pray. It's prayer that puts the power within us to work.

The Holy Spirit is in us and He's waiting on us! He's ready anytime, day and night. He is saying,

"I am here to help you, to strengthen you and to lead you. I want to comfort you today. You know that problem you've been facing and the challenges that you encounter daily? I want to help you with that. I want to help you get that out of your life." The Holy Spirit has things He desires to show each of us. Things we've been trying to figure out. He's waiting to help us overcome every obstacle in our life. Ask Him for His help each and every day. Take time to pray in the Spirit. Your prayers activate the power that is at work within you.

Act 4:5-12 "When Peter and John stood accused before powerful leaders, Luke reported that Peter was filled with the Holy Spirit and boldly proclaimed that Jesus Christ of Nazareth, the One they had crucified, was the only way to salvation. This is the same Peter who only two months earlier had denied Jesus. And now, standing in the very place where Jesus had been condemned, Peter accused these religious elite that they had crucified the Messiah. That new boldness could only be possible through the empowering of the Holy Spirit.

Listen people of God, the power of the Holy Spirit is very important to every believer or follower of Jesus Christ . We need this power to fulfill the purpose that Jesus started and left the finishing part for us to accomplish."

We all know that Christians in the first century faced great afflictions. They endured severe testing, hard times, persecutions that were life-and-death. But they didn't break down under the stress. They kept the good fight of faith.

I have seen the same power changing my life and everything that attached to me. I have seen people's life changed for good, people receiving blessings and breakthrough in every areas of their lives. I have seen healing taking place to believers and unbelievers too. When you are empowered with this power, there will be absolutely nothing to stop you or stop what God is doing in your life. God wants to help you live a productive life.

The power of the Holy Spirit will be able to turn your life around from curses to blessings and abundant life, from rejections to acceptance, from a lower life to a higher life and so on.

And it is through the power of the Holy Spirit within us that we can gain spiritual understanding and insight. Corinthians 2:11-12 say;

"For what man knows the things of a ma except [by] the spirit of the man which is in Him? Even so no one knows the things of God except [by] the Spirit of God."

Jesus Christ told His followers that the Holy Spirit which the Father would send to them will guide them and be with them in His absence.

"Will teach you all things, and bring to your remembrance all things that I said to you (John 14:26)

You can see the divine inspiration and divine understanding and wisdom we gain when we walk with Holy Spirit. He fills us up. The bible also shows that God inspires and guides His prophets and servants through the power of the Holy Spirit. Peter said from the book 2 Peter 1:21; "Prophecy never came by the will of man, but holy men of God spoke as they were moved by the Holy Spirit."

As I am writing this chapter, I see the power of the Holy Ghost ministering to you right now, trying to correct every mark that was left on your life and failure that was spoken and attributed to you. He is removing all that from you now. He is anointing you with His divine power. As God anointed Jesus of Nazareth with the Holy Spirit and power and Jesus went about doing good and healing all who were oppressed by the devil, and performed mighty miracles during His earthly call, He is doing the same to your life now.

He is writing a new chapter and putting a new desire of wanting Him and His power.

Thank you, Jesus. We love you Lord!

This power is real, and it is through the Holy Spirit's teachings and guiding power that we are sealed and confirmed until the day of redemption.

The power of the Holy Spirit will not work until we put it to work! Take time to pray in the Spirit. Your prayers activate the power that is at work within you.

Chapter 3

Why you need the power of the Holy Spirit

The bible presents the role of the Holy Spirit as a continuation of the work of God the Father and Jesus Christ, the Son in the lives of the believer. As such, He is an essential companion of every Christian and is the guarantee and means by which we persevere to the point of reaching Heaven. Let me further explain this to gives us a deeper understanding.

Many Christians today get caught and forget the importance of the Holy Spirit. Many others know Jesus and the Father but fewer know the Holy Spirit or have a relationship with Him in their daily lives. The truth is, the Holy Spirit is the real POWER of God that will revolutionize our lives if we'll let Him in to lead us. Listen, if we want to avoid being "powerless spiritually," we need to respond to the Holy Spirit and the way He moves in our lives.

Luke 1:35 - The angel answered and said to her, The Holy Spirit will come upon you, and the power of the Most High will overshadow you; and for that reason the holy Child shall be called the Son of God.

He empowers us to do what is right, live in faith and do good works (Rom 7:18, Eph 2:4-10). It is always God's work in us that means that we are saved in Christ and living new lives for Him. It is the Spirit that makes Christians aware of their sins and empowers them to turn away from them in repentance.

We need the Holy Spirit more than we know Him. Here are the reasons why we should cry out for more of Him:

1. The Holy Spirit helps us build our faith.

Jude 20 says, "But you, beloved, build yourselves up in your most holy faith. Pray in the Holy Spirit." I pray in the Spirit for at least the first 30 minutes of my day and pray in spirit in spurts throughout the day. I am praying in the Spirit as I write this article. I am edifying my spirit man when I do this.

2. The Holy Spirit gives us supernatural power. Jesus said in Acts 1:8, "But you shall receive power when the Holy Spirit comes upon you. And you shall be My witnesses in Jerusalem, and in all Judea and Samaria, and to the ends of the earth." Right about now should be when you should cry out, "Holy Spirit, come upon me. Fill me again and again.

3. The Holy Spirit helps us resist temptation. Romans 8:13 says, "For if you live according to the flesh, you will die, but if through the Spirit you put to death the deeds of the body, you will live." And Galatians 5:16 says, "I say then, walk in the Spirit, and you shall not fulfill the lust of the flesh." If you are struggling with temptation of any kind, ask the

Holy Spirit to help you. He is your helper. He's right there waiting for you to ask.

4. He guarantees your hope of Heaven. The Holy Spirit is also important because He is the guarantee of your inheritance in Heaven. "When you believed, you were marked in Him with a seal, the promised Holy Spirit who is a deposit guaranteeing our inheritance until the redemption of those who are God's possession" (Ephesians 1:13-14). Satan wants to destroy your hope and tries to get you to doubt your Savior's love. But the Spirit's leading, teaching, gifting, and proclaiming is a proof that you belong to God forever.

5. The Holy Spirit gives new life, the Bible says that we are dead in our sins and trespassing Ephesians 2:1

6. The Holy Spirit gives you power to serve Christ. Act 1:8-You will receive power when the Holy Spirit comes on you and you will be my witness.

In my opinion, many believers today haven't experienced deliverance or breakthrough because they are holding onto their own plans and not letting the Holy Spirit in. That's it.

John 1:16; Moreover, the Holy Spirit is not fully received until he is fully in charge. We simply haven't received if we haven't given him complete CONTROL over our lives. We have to cast ourselves totally into His care and let Him lead.

If you are ready and willing to let the Holy Spirit lead and guide you, I promise you that the Holy Spirit will turn your situations around and be able to walk on His anointing for His glory. Yes, there is darkness all around, but you have received the light of the Holy Spirit, the power of God is in you. He will turn the darkness before you into light, the rough places into level ground.

John 12:46, I have come to the world as a light, so that whoever believes in me may not remain in darkness.

Matthew 5:16, In the way, let your light shine before others, so that they may see your good works and give glory to your Father who is in heaven.

The Holy Spirit is the real POWER of God that will revolutionize our lives if we'll let Him.

"Be empowered and controlled by the Holy Spirit as a way of life from now and forever more."

CHAPTER 4

Where do you want to be spiritually?

Ask yourself, do you really want to grow and become who you should be in the kingdom of God? Although, God can use people after they have become born again to do great things, not everyone reaches their maximum potential. You know why? I'm convinced they don't want it badly enough. You have to be hungry and thirsty enough to ask God to fulfill the promises and prophecies that He spoke over your life. Some people do just enough to get by while others are driven to reach their goals. Which of the groups do you belong to?

If you want to separate yourself from the average believer, you need to develop a better appetite, to have a hunger to succeed that's beyond normal and be willing to exceed your limit which is almost an obsession. Start to build your life on what God wants, put your priorities in the correct order. You have to keep in mind that God always rewards, so therefore, continue to be faithful to Him and do not look on what people say about you or about your situation. Do not let fear keep you from reaching your potentials and destiny.

King David said, *"I have been young, and now am old, yet I have not seen the righteous forsake, his descendants begging bread."* (Psalm 37:25)

Over his entire lifetime, King David had never seen God's servant out begging for bread. We all know the story of Lot's wife. Lot's wife disregarded the admonition and "she looked from behind, and she became a pillar of salt (Genesis 19:26).

Many Christian lose focus on the way and forget completely the instructions that God has given to them. Suddenly, confusion and temptation sets in and they begin to lose appetite for the things of God. You have to know that there are so many things in this world that fight for our time, and they can come in the form of money, job, car and so on. And when we allow them to take too much control "we are finished." We have to fight back to stay focused by keeping this instructions and activities in check.

In this journey of growing, you will go through different times. Difficult times where things may seem like they are not moving, no hope, combined with one challenge after another, one temptation after another. Let this not stop you from going where God wants you to be or doing what God is telling you to do .The Lord always will come through to rescue His people. He knows that we need Him every time and every hour. He knows that there's nothing we can accomplish without Him being on our side. So, you have to understand the season you're in and always ask the Holy Spirit to help you and lead you at all time.

Ecclesiastes 3:1-8 says, "To Everything there is a season, A time for every purpose under heaven." Put in mind, growing is the PROCESS and you can not skip the process. Many people in the Bible were able to reached to their destination only because they believed in God that all things are possible, With God on their side, they can do anything.

I'm encouraging you today, no matter your age, background or your experience, you're only limited by your own unbelief. God is able to do exceedingly abundantly above all that we ask or think, according to the power that works in us. Let me share with you the tips I've been using to stay focused, and I believe as you apply them faithfully, they are going to help you too.

1. Read bible

James 1:23-25 declares, "Anyone who listens to the word but does not do what it says is like a man who looks at his face in a mirror and, after looking at himself, goes away and immediately forgets what he looks like. But the man who looks intently into the perfect law that gives freedom, and continues to do this, not forgetting what he has heard, but doing it - he will be blessed in what he do.

2 Timothy 3:16-17 teaches us, "All Scripture is God-breathed and is useful for teaching, rebuking, correcting and training in righteousness, so that the man of God may be thoroughly equipped for every good work.

Our focus should not be on comparing ourselves with others rather we should compare ourselves with God's Word. The Scriptures are the mirror to show us what we are like spiritually and to shine light in the areas that needs to experience and learn spiritual growth.

2. Read books that will help you grow

When I made up my mind that I wanted to grow, my greatest ambition was to please the Lord, the reason I learned more about God and I lived right following Him in truth and in spirit. Because I know and I He will make my life successful. And being successful means to fulfill God's calling on my life.

3. Pick someone you admire and let them be your guide or mentor.

You need a mentor who is willing to share his wisdom and experience with you at all times. Ask someone who has already been successful to guide you. This will boost your confidence. In the book of 2 Kings 2:

The prophet Elisha was followed the prophet Elijah from town to town, watching and learning from Elijah. Elijah asked Elisha, "What do you want from me?"

Elisha replied, "I want a double portion of your power."

"If you watch me go, you will get it," Elijah replied.

When Elijah took off in his chariot, Elisha received Elijah's power. What are you learning from Elisha? This is what I have learned; if you want something so bad, you will have to stick with the person who has been through that phase and succeeded in it. Period.

4. Don't hold back to tap into people who have inspired you and use their energy in guiding your way.

This principle is working wonderfully well. If you are obsessed with doing your best, always be ready to learn from guys who have already done it.

5. Pay attention to the things you'd normally brush off as coincidences.

I view coincidence as an added advantage. Be wise enough not to ignore things and also be wise enough to listen to wise people. I've gained wisdoms, insight and knowledge from this way.

6. Pay attention to your dreams.

I noticed God teaches, speaks and warn His people in dream so often. Like me, I learnt a lot from God and I'm still learning through dreams. He thought me so many things with regards to "The power of the Holy Spirit." That's when I started to be serious with all the dreams that I dream.

7. Habit

Make a habit of telling people why you like them and how they make your life better. After having my encounter with Jesus, my attitude changed entirely. I always want to make people feel better by sharing positive messages and helping causes.

8. Forgive

Forgive people you've been holding grudges against. Letting go of anger doesn't have to mean accepting what someone did to you or saying that they were right, it's just about getting those negative feelings out of your body so that they don't weigh so heavily on you.

9. Fast

Take a fast once in a week to dedicate your body, mind and soul to your master as a living sacrifice. Fast will help you to focus on God. It depends on your ability, you can do for more days.

10. Journal

Every day start by thinking of two or three things you're grateful for. Write them down and think of how you can deal with them spiritually.

The book psalm says, surely goodness and mercy shall fall on me all the days of my life. God promises that goodness and mercy will follow us for the whole life. So, instead of worrying and complaining.

Try to live one day at time, enjoying each moment and trust God for provision for the things you need.

11. Pray

Having one on one time with God is very important. Prayer will bring the biggest fire in your spiritual life. Jesus taught us to pray "Give us this day our daily bread," it's called daily bread because God wants us to live one day at a time. He didn't tell us to pray for yearly bread. God wants us to trust Him on our daily basis.

12. Meditate

Meditate on the word of God to turn off the part of your brain that is critical and overly logical and allow God to speak to you. And this will discipline your mind to focus on God no matter what happens.

13. Walk in Spirit.

Without the Holy Spirit in us, we will not know where we are going or what we are doing. So be willing to follow His directions at all times. Refuse to do things on your ways rather look up to Him and follow His ways as He was given to us. He is waiting for you to ask Him "Holy spirit I can't do without you."

"It's God's plan for every believer to grow from spiritual infancy to spiritual maturity."

"Let the word of Christ dwell in you richly in all wisdom, teaching and admonishing one another with psalms, hymns and spiritual songs, singing with grace in your heart to God."

CHAPTER 5

Who is qualified to go with you?

If you need to be your BEST, you must get rid of the negative people or things that are weighing you down. Yes, you to decide! That extra weight will slow you down and keep you from reaching your destination, you've got to let it go. Examine yourself if you have an excess luggage that's killing you because this might be a bad habit or a bad company that need to be broken.

You know yourself and your addiction. Is it a smoking, drinking, gossiping, cheating or unhealthy eating habit? Are you involving in ungodly relationship? Whether you know it or not that you're carrying that person, people or things around on your back, they will certainly weigh you down. And you will never be able to move up when you're holding those things or people.

I believe God has a plan for everyone including you and me. He has placed us on earth for a reason, but we won't discover it until we decide to look on Him. God has wonderfully made you and He has a good plan for you. He wants the best for you. He will never let you follow any suggestion that points you down the wrong road.

God knows there some bad spiritual advice out there that might push you further away from Him. That's why He wants us to pay extra attention to the people we are surrounding ourselves with. We have to test every spirit, every word and every advice if it's lining up with the word of God. One of my favorites is, **1 John 4; Dear friend, do not believe every spirit, but test the spirit to whether they are from God. Because Many false prophets have gone out into the world.**

When I was growing up, my mother taught me that it is better to walk away from the wrong people than to support them. She believes if you hang out with the wrong people, you'll soon become like them, which is very true! Because of her good advice and many tidbits wisdom, I am who I am today. I have never been in any fights or been the center of any drama in my life. I'm happy she also taught me to respect others but also to be wise. So, carrying my mother's advice and God on my side, I find peace in myself. Because I know that God will not let me fall into the wrong hands and I don't make up any excuses for both myself and God when it comes to the point of choosing my CIRCLE.

The first verse in the Psalm 1:1 "Blessed in the man who walks not in the counsel of the ungodly, nor sin the path of sinners, nor sits in the seat of the scornful."

I have come to realize that God blesses people when they LISTEN and are READY to walk with Him. The people that are not driven by any other force than the Spirit of God. It doesn't matter what other people say about you, no matter what criticism or judgment they may pass against you, always bear in mind that you are a child of God. You do not have to be affected by their opinions or their views. Be silent and wait for the Lord.

Psalm 37:7 says, Be still in the presence of the Lord, and wait patiently for him to act. Don't worry about evil people who prosper or fret about their wicked schemes.

God wants to use us in ways we can't imagine. So, use your time and energy well to build your inner world. Remember, you can't go His way and your way at the same. My personal view is, **"if I make the right decision every day, I'll always be pleased with the results later. And if I sow a good seed, I'll reap a good harvest."**

Here are my tips I use to know if the person is qualified to go with me. And my number **ONE** tip is, does the person has the fruits of the spirit? These are the fruits that all Christians should be producing in their new lives with Jesus Christ.

1.   Fruit of the Spirit - Visible Growth in Jesus Christ.

"Fruit of the Spirit" is a biblical term that sums up the nine visible attributes of a true Christian life.

Galatians 5:22-23, these attributes are: love, joy, peace, longsuffering, gentleness, goodness, faith, meekness and temperance. We learn from the scripture that these are not individual "fruits" from which we pick and choose. Rather, the fruit of the Spirit is one nine-fold "fruit" that characterizes all who truly walk in the Holy Spirit.

Love - "And so we know and rely on the love God has for us. God is love. Whoever lives in love lives in God, and God in him" (1 John 4:16). Through Jesus Christ, our greatest goal is to do all things in love. "Love is patient, love is kind. It does not envy, it does not boast, it is not proud rather love is humble. It is not rude, it is not self-seeking, it is not easily angered, and it keeps no record of wrongs. Love does not have delight in evil but rejoices with the truth. It always protects, trusts, hopes, and perseveres. Love never fails."

Joy - "The joy of the Lord is your strength" (Nehemiah 8:10). "Let us fix our eyes on Jesus, the author and finisher of our faith, who for the joy set before Him endured the cross, scorning and its shame, and sat down at the right hand of the throne of God" (Hebrews 12:2).

Peace - "Therefore, since we have been justified through faith, we have peace with God through our Lord Jesus Christ" (Romans 5:1). "May the God of hope fill you with all joy and peace as you trust in Him so that you may overflow with hope by the power of the Holy Spirit" (Romans 15:13).

Longsuffering (patience) - We are "strengthened with all might, according to His glorious power, unto all patience and longsuffering with joyfulness" (Colossians 1:11). "With all lowliness and meekness, with longsuffering, forbearing one another in love" (Ephesians 4:2).

Gentleness (kindness) - We should live "in purity, understanding, patience and kindness in the Holy Spirit and in sincere love, in truthful speech and in the power of God with weapons of righteousness in the right hand and in the left" (2 Corinthians 6:6-7).

Goodness - "Wherefore also we pray always for you, that our God would count you worthy of this calling and fulfill all the good pleasure of His goodness, and the work of faith with power" (2 Thessalonians 1:11). "For the fruit of the Spirit is in all goodness and righteousness and truth" (Ephesians 5:9).

Faith (faithfulness) - "O Lord, thou art my God, I will exalt thee, I will praise thy name for thou hast done wonderful things. Thy counsels of old are faithfulness and truth" (Isaiah 25:1). "I pray that out of His glorious riches that He may strengthen you with power through His Spirit in your inner being, so that Christ may dwell in your hearts through faith" (Ephesians 3:16-17).

Meekness - "Brethren, if a man be overtaken in a fault, ye which are spiritual, restore such a person in the spirit of meekness; considering thyself, lest thou also be tempted" (Galatians 6:1). "With all lowliness and meekness, with longsuffering, forbearing one another in love."

Remember you died with Christ and have crucified the flesh. Your life needs to represent Jesus all the time. Look at this verse and those who belong to Christ Jesus have crucified the flesh with its passions and desires (Galatians 5:24).

You need to start asking yourself what relationships or friendships that you keep that are not giving God glory. Then, pull back, tell them about your faith and what you stand for when it comes to your faith. Do you know that you need to protect the power of the Holy Spirit that God has installed in you? Because guess what? If you don't do it and keep entertaining bad company, the power will leave you at once for it doesn't dwell in unrighteousness. The Holy Spirit doesn't stay in a dirty place. The bible says, our body is the temple of God. My advice to you is;

Be friends with spiritually minded people. Whoever walks with the wise becomes wise, but the companion of fools will suffer harm. (Proverbs 13:20) Do not be deceived: "Bad company ruins good morals." (1 Corinthians 15:33)

SECOND, does the person have the qualifications of a good spiritual partner? And how can I know?

1. Follows Jesus

If you can't tell that your Spiritual mentor is following Jesus, then how can you be sure that she is going to teach you to follow Jesus? Paul tells the Church at Galatia that evidence, or fruit of being filled with the Holy Spirit is that a person demonstrates love, joy, peace, patience.

2. Trustworthy

If you can't trust your partner, then you will never share the total truth with him/her. If you can't be honest, then you will never meet your spiritual goals.

Proverbs 11:13 says; **"No one who gossips can be trusted with a secret, but you can put confidence in someone who is trustworthy. It's the gossip-check game. If it fails there is no chance a partnering relationship would work"**.

3. Raw honesty

If your partner can't tell you the truth, even if that truth hurts your feelings, then it will do you zero good. A good partner can offend you compassionately. Sometimes, we need to hear the raw truth about ourselves to shock us out of denial.

Now, your partner tells you the truth, you must humbly accept the truth even if it hurts. Of course, the truth is more easily accepted if you know your partner has your best interest in mind and is not serving a selfish agenda. This also means that your partner is not afraid to ask you difficult questions that makes you feel uncomfortable.

4. Advice

Your partner needs to help cultivate the work of the Holy Spirit in you for the plans that God has for you to materialize. Sometimes, partners can give poor advice because they unknowingly are serving an agenda to fill "needs". They want to mold you into what the group needs and not what God is calling you to do. So be careful. A good partner will help you to identify the areas in your life where you feel God wants to address and will work from that list not otherwise.

5. Humility

A good spiritual partner will constantly be pointing to how Jesus has dealt with the brokenness of life. The stories will revolve around God's grace and mercy being revealed in the midst of personal doubt and despair. Jesus will be the reason for the victory over sin, and not personal willpower and strength. This is true humility, "I know where my help comes from."

6. Patience

You will test the limits of your partner's patience. A good spiritual partner will see the breakthrough you are about to make and patiently wait for you to make it. While it seems so close to your partner, it may seem miles away to you. Your partner will patiently wait for the Spirit to help you close that gap. Amen!

7. Build on common interests

There is usually something that draws people together — a common hobby, a sport, a Bible study, a volunteer project, a children's activity. If we take advantage of the common activities and interests we have with others, we can fit the time for friendship into our schedules. If you and a friend both like to exercise, work out together, if you both like to read, go to the bookstore together to pick out your next selection, grab some coffee, and talk about the last book you read. If your kids are your common interest, consider getting together on a regular basis to pray for them. The point is to allow your common interests to draw you together and the bond will be established.

Colossians 3:13 says; Bear with each other and forgive one another if any of you has a grievance against someone. Forgive as the Lord forgave you.

8. Appreciate the differences in others.

God created people with a variety of personalities, talents, and interests. Each one of us is a unique creation. When mixed together, we blend to form the body of Christ.

The truth is, we will never find a perfect friend here on this earth (except Jesus). So let's appreciate our differences, both the good and the bad.

9. A positive person.

People who bring you down with their problems and complaints are generally not the ones you want to hang around with for any length of time. Of course, sometimes a friend will go through a difficult time, and we need to be ready and willing to hold a hand and provide a listening ear to such person. But a friend in need is different than a habitual whiner. We want our friendships to be positive and uplifting, and that means we must be positive because while uplifting friends ourselves.

10. A giver, not a taker

Giving and self-sacrifice are part of the definition of love. What can we give to others? How about a smile, a hug, a kind word, a listening ear, help with a task, a prayer, an encouraging note, a meal? We can come up with many things to give to others if we are willing to be attentive to their needs.

Choosing your circle wisely is very important!

As positive women, we need to make sure our tongues are used for good and not evil. We should be builders with our words, not demolishers.

CHAPTER 6

What are your goals, plans, and vision?

Let me break this down so we can all flow together. Vision from a biblical perspective:

Proverbs 29:18 **"Where there is no vision, the people are unrestrained, but happy is he who keeps the law."**

Vision is the bridge between the present and the future. Without it, we perish or go "unrestrained," just as the New American Standard Bible puts it.

What is the goal from bible perspective?

Goals are the "map" that will guide you toward your God-given purpose, without setting them, you will also wander in circles without getting where you want to go. The life becomes stagnant.

What is the plan?

Bible says from Proverbs 16:3, Commit to the Lord whatever you do, and he will establish your plans.

Also, Jeremiah 29:11,For I know the plans I have for you, declares the Lord, plans for welfare and not for evil, to give you a future and hope.

Listen, you can have many plans but does your plans bring God glory? Do they honor him? Those are the questions you need to ask.

We may make our plan, but God has the last word and answer. You may think everything you do is right, but the LORD judges our motives. Make sure you plan with God and ask Him to bless your plan. You know, when we don't put Him into account, we put ourselves into circumstances that are not God's plan for us and suddenly, we realize that we have been making our plans without Him, that we have not even considered Him to be a vital. I suggest you sit down with God and evaluate yourself. For example, if it is a reading habit, set some reading plans for the year to ensure that during the time you're engaging fully with Him. Another question to ask:

What efforts are you putting to involve God into your plans?

Access yourself to know whether it's spiritual issues or practical issues. Many Christians think it is inappropriate or unnecessary to put God first, but this is not true. We must go to God as we are and remember these conditions when you plan in order for Him to extend His favor upon your plans.

- Don't plan without Him even in your everyday issues of life.
- Don't plan with a concern for evil in mind.

Veronica Abisay

God created you and every person on Earth with several parts to function differently. Like a pie with separate pieces, each part is critical to who you are and all of these parts must be considered when you set goals.

Spiritual, Family, Social, Physical, Work.

If you fail to give each part the proper attention and care as you reach toward your God-given purpose, you'll experience problems, and this may lead to depression of the soul. God created us as a spiritual being, He wants us to love Him with our whole heart, soul and mind. This means that your goals must agree with your spiritual convictions. If you set goals that goes against what God asks of you, you will become fragmented emotionally and intellectually and you will lose your joy and enthusiasm. Because God created you to need connection with others, if you neglect the social aspect of your life and become an "all work and no play," you will become out of balance and you'll most likely experience physical, emotional, social and spiritual troubles.

There's no doubt that God wants you to fulfill your purpose on earth. In fact, it's your duty since He has given you gifts to do so. However, be mindful not to neglect any of the five areas that makes up who you are while you do His work and watch what God will do for you! Finally, remember that the world does not rest on your shoulders. You will make mistakes in setting goals. It's OK. Because God wants to see you do His will, He will teach you the way to go as you walk in faith (Psalm 32:8). You must say to yourself, my best days are still ahead as stated in

57

Jeremiah 29:11, For I know the plans I have for you, declares the Lord plans for welfare and not for evil, to give a future and a hope.

So, commit your goals to God, and note that for every believer it is very important to do so. The bible promises us that He is always present when we need Him, and He will never forsake us. The bible also shows us that God care about every aspect of our lives and he wants to be a part of it. Let God give you the strength and guidance you need as you commune with Him in daily reading of His word and prayer and watch Him help you to realize your dreams.

Let's go deeper. Ask yourself where you want to be in your relationship with the Lord by the end of the year and then set tangible goals for getting there and work hard to achieve them. Bible says, **"Without prophetic vision, the people shall perish, but he that keeps the law is blessed."**

This is not only going to help you not to be a sponge or a baby in Christ, but also will help you to enjoy the sweetness of Christ and working in your destiny confidently. Creating steps to progress with your goals is very important to any believer who wants to grow, sit down with God and set some spiritual goals for the next year to ensure that during the time you're staying in your goals. Too many believers want to get the prize without having to sacrifice anything. It just doesn't happen that way. You can't be a great minister without goals and commitment.

And put this in mind, no matter how many attachments you have in your life, when you set goals you'll have to stay on top of your goals and determine to do with excellence. No matter how significant any assignment may be, it can never become more important than God. If it ever does, the task automatically turns into an idol. The only way to prevent idolatry is to love the Lord with all of your heart and follow His teachings.

I have some examples of spiritual goals that you can set through the years to keep you in track with God as you fulfill your God-given purpose. I recommend only choosing 2-3 for the year to prevent overwhelming yourself and suddenly becomes a task to carry out. You can always add more as you complete them!

1. **Stay committed**

Whenever you feel like you can't make it or have made several mistakes, sit down and remember why you started in the first place, what you hope to achieve, why and what it will do for you spiritual growth if you should have it. If you give up, how will it affect your spiritual growth too.

2. **Read books that will help you grow.**

Set a goal to read a book every month, or every three months, or whatever is realistic for you. Also, consider reading books that will challenge and convict you internally and externally...that's where the growth comes.

3.   Restore someone's faith

Today, make time to heal a wounded heart, to extend kindness to someone who really needs a friend, or to help gather up pieces of a broken dream. Today, do whatever you can to radiate God's unconditional love.

4.   Count your blessings

Record your blessings and answered prayers. Keep a "blessing book" in which you record every blessing that comes your way throughout the year, adding a prayer of thanks or praise.

 In addition, write out your prayer requests and record the answers as they are answered by God. By writing out these types of things, you will not only be more keenly aware of how God is working in and around your life, but you will be able to see your progress in becoming one who does "everything without complaining or arguing. (Philippians 2:14) and a person who gives thanks in all circumstances."

5.   Pick a "Theme verse"

Pick a theme verse for the year and say it aloud every day that passes by. I guarantee if you do this, by the end of the year and probably a lot sooner, you will have memorized that verse. And that's one more verse in the Word of God that you will have memorized during your lifetime.

Make some of these action points your priority in life this time next year and hopefully by the end of 2019, I will be able to testify God's victory in your life. I have seen this change my life like nobody's business. My theme for the year 2018 is:

"From the time of John Baptist until now, the kingdom of God suffers violence and the violent take it by force-Matthew 11:12.

6. Study a Topic

Ask yourself where you want to be in your relationship with the Lord by the end of the year and then set tangible goals in achieving and getting there. For instance, if you want to know Him better, consider a study of His names in the Old Testament and Jesus' "I am" statements in the New Testament. If you need to slow down and learn how to listen to His voice, study all the Word says about "rest" or "hearing" or His "voice." If there are characters or traits you know you need to work on, consider an in-depth study of some or all of the fruits of the spirit (Galatians 5:22-23).

7. Share the Journey

Start a weekly prayer group with others who share similar concerns and motives in your heart. (For example, praying with other moms for your children, praying with other wives for unsaved spouses, praying during your lunch hour with co-workers, or praying with friends or church members for a specific burden God has placed on your heart).

8. Journal

Start a journal to record your growth. Start journaling your thoughts as you read the Word of God. How did a certain passage compel you to pray? What changes are you asking God to make in your life? What discoveries have you made about His character or His Word? Date each page. By the end of the year, you'll have a record of where God took you and what He has shown you through the past 12 months.

9. Disciple a new believer

We learn the most when we teach extensively to others about what we know. It entails the sharing of knowledge. And seeing them grasp the truth for the first time gives it a fresh impact on our lives as well.

10. Meditate on scripture

The Bible is loaded with verses of comfort, encouragement, and wisdom. Make it a habit to read and study your Bible in a regular, and disciplined way. Highlight verses that speak to you. Meditate on those words. Memorize some of the passages so that you can recall them from memory at a future time.

11. Fast and Pray

Prayer linked with fasting was often done by people in the Bible. Ezra 8:23 reports: "So we fasted and earnestly prayed that our God would take care of us, and he heard our prayer." The next time you are asked to pray urgently for someone in difficulty, consider combining your praying with some fasting. This will do the trick and lead you to the solution.

12. Strive for Excellence

The Bible tells us: "Whatever you do, do well" (Ecclesiastes 9:10). Be the best that you can be at whatever station you are in life in which God has placed you.

13. Be reliable

Do what you say you will do, whether it's convenient or not. Follow through on all of your commitments, large and small. By your actions, show others you are a person who can be trusted and counted upon in any situation.

14. Ask God to make you a blessing

A great way to grow in wonder and amazement is by asking God to turn your life into a blessing. Do this each morning before resuming your daily activities. Offer a short, simple prayer like this one: "Dear God, on this day, make my life a blessing to someone, somewhere." Then, pay close attention to every person you encounter during the day, as God will honor your prayer, sometimes it will come in surprising ways.

15. Keep your priorities straight

Know what is ultimately important and what is not.

16. Spread love wherever you go

"Spread love everywhere you go: First of all in your own house. Let no one ever come to you without leaving better and happier. Be the living expression of God's kindness; kindness in your face, kindness in your eyes, kindness in your smile, kindness in your warm greeting." They will certainly see you as light.

17. Serve

Look for ways to serve the community, especially tasks that promise no reward, such as volunteering in hospitals or schools. Read and reflect on the action of Jesus in John 13:1-5.

18. Allow Spirit to lead

Spiritual growth means taking a leap of faith from time to time rather than trying to get everything in place before you start something important, why not follow God's leading and allow the plan to evolve? This means taking a step of faith and trusting God to provide what may be needed for success to be achieved.

19. Healthy Conversation

Have a conversation with people who have experiences, with what you want to know more about or with people who have been there.

20. Find Inspiration

Discuss or explain spiritual concepts, practices, or inspiring words with someone.

21. Do what you enjoy (hobbies)

If you like singing, playing instruments, teaching kids, preaching or evangelism, it will be a wise decision to join the department and be open to learn.

22. Listen to online sermons and live streams

Watch and listen to different good Christian sermons online that will help you grow. What spiritual goals do you want to make and what obstacles do you think you will face? Or what spiritual goals are you working on now and what obstacles are you currently facing to seeing your goals come to pass? Please write them down, it will help you to stay focused to achieve all your dreams and heart desires.

"Commit to the Lord whatever you do, and he will establish your plans."

"Without prophetic vision, the people shall perish, but he that keeps the law is blessed."

CHAPTER 7

Five Keys to Success

When I first made up my mind that I don't want to be an average follower of Jesus Christ, I decided I was going to do whatever it takes for me to learn a new and different ways to become successful both spiritually and physically. First, let's see what it means when I say, "physical success." Physical Success is achieved not only by big plans or complicated goals but by simple common-sense actions and by being obedient to God. Let me point out that being successful, or poor is a choice we make, whether you find yourself in a world of economic stress and strife or in a world of economic abundance and wellness. I know this can be a big challenge for many of you, but Holy Spirit will help you to understand.

Deuteronomy 15:4-5, **"There must be no poor people among you because God is going to bless you lavishly in this land that God, your God, is giving you as an inheritance, you very own land. But only if you listen obediently to the Voice of God, your God, diligently observing every commandment that I command you today."**

Deuteronomy 27:12, **"The LORD will open the heavens the storehouse of his bounty, to send rain on your land in season and to bless all the work of your hands. You will lend to many nations but will borrow from none"**

The scriptures say that God will bless us but we must diligently follow His commandments or His instructions. You can see now that poverty is not godly and certainly isn't biblical. God wants us to open our eyes to see the invisible world, to see the blessings He has in store for all those who love Him. So "being poor is a choice." PERIOD!

Our inheritance as sons and daughters of the King of all kings is a life free from want and poverty. I have seen so many unsaved successful people who follow biblical principles, yet they just don't realize they came from the Bible.

One night as I was getting ready to seek the face of God, the Holy Spirit led me to some scriptures that was talking about being successful in a spiritual path. I felt so angry with myself and asked why do I live this type of life? God's word doesn't advocate poverty for anyone. So why do I keep entertaining it? I heard a voice say, "Is time to FIGHT" and take your total control of your financial destiny. So, I told devil right away, your time has EXPIRED. So therefore, I'm here to declare to you that ENOUGH is ENOUGH. I was so tired of calling myself a born again Christian but still suffering in poverty, chronic back pain, migraine and so on. I'm taking back everything that you stole and took from me either with my permission or without my permission.

Whether it my prayer life, my way of giving and serving God, my commitment and dedication to the Lord, my breakthrough, my blessings, my marriage, my joy, I'm coming out aggressively and am taking them back NOW. I took my journal and pen and wrote down everything that was missing from me. I also asked the Holy Spirit to remind me if there's anything that I needed to write down. Oh, he did answer!

The next day, I called one of my spiritual partners, and explained to her the whole revelation. I continued to talk toward my plan that is "To fight back." I made up my mind that I want to see God's glory and overflow in every area of my life. I know that my greatest ambition is to please the Lord at all times. That's why I learn more about God, that's why I pray, that's why I live right. But I need to have a better life. I believe God can bless me. The bible says, "Blessed is the man who walks not in the counsel of the ungodly. In the law he meditates day and night. It means, I am BLESSED already. I shouted out! I'm tired. I refuse the poverty mentality from my life in Jesus name. I know God can change my story in a second if I follow His commandments.

3 John 1:2"Beloved, I pray that in every way you may prosper and enjoy good health, as your soul also prospers.

So, my spiritual partner told me, "You are in your best moment." I feel you, I have never seen you talk like this before. She kept saying, "You know God has a plan for us, and that it is a good one. God let you see that because He wants you to be prosperous, but the devil wanted you to be poor." She said to me, "If something is worth doing, it is worth doing it right. So, let's ask God for the instructions and I said OK.

It is very important to have godly and wise people around you, people you can choose to call friends, partners, mentors, you can also choose to call whoever a name you want that works best for you.

Remember our successful life begins by acknowledging God as number one of our priority list. Jesus said, "But seek first the kingdom of God and His righteousness, and all these things shall be added to you." When you allow God to rule your life, He will provide everything else that you need. When God becomes your top priority, you will be amazed at how the other areas of your life will straighten out.

I had a dream one night where I saw two angels holding my hands and showing me the blueprint of my destiny. They were explaining to me what my assignment on this earth is all about and they came to assure me that am not alone, and that they will always be with me because they have been assigned to help me fulfill my purpose. After one week, the Holy Spirit led us to take fast for forty days. We were eating fruits, vegetables and drinking a lot of water. It was tough at first, going without food, avoiding those delicious food my husband knows how to make and all that. After two weeks, I lost over fifteen pounds. At this point my husband thought it was too much for me.

On the twentieth day of the fasting program, God started revealing truths to me as I read the Bible and pray daily. I started noticing my tongue changed for I was praying I was praying with new tongues. Each day that passes by, I was noticing new power bestowed in me. God told me, Veronica, I anointed you to carry my glory, I have a great task for you my daughter.

So, I want to strengthen your spirits. This fasting will prepare you to enter holy of holies place. l will teach and show you things and revelations that you have never seen or experienced in your entire life as a believer. You will be victorious over sin and carry my glory with you. He took me to the book of

Matthew 4:1 says that Jesus was led by the Holy Spirit into the wilderness to fast for forty days and nights. During that time of fasting, Jesus was repeatedly tempted by the devil. This testing time prepared Him for the three-year ministry that would change the world. If the son of God Jesus Christ did so you will and can also do it. I said yes Lord! By the fortieth fast day, I had lost approximately 30 pounds. But I came out powerful and unstoppable, God honored my fast in another way that I wasn't expecting. He opened doors of opportunities and brought unto me the power of connections.

Another good thing came out of my fast was that God gave me 5 keys to unlock my blessings. If you use them faithfully you will see specific changes in your life too. Let me answer this question first, many people ask, "What is key to success?" That's a simple question for me to answer. Success always comes as a result of doing things that are right and staying away from the things that brings failure. God can make anyone successful, but He has conditions for extending His favor.

1. God doesn't reward lazy people. The book of Matthew 11:12 says, From the days of John the Baptist until now the day of Veronica Swai the kingdom of heaven suffers violence, and violence men take it by force.

2. God doesn't reward people who give up too soon.

God's promises are yes and amen, and His goodness is promised for those who wait patiently for Him no matter how long it will take. (Psalm 40:1)

3. God doesn't reward people who are weak.

Exodus 14:15 says, The Lord will fight for you but you need to be STILL, Also the Bible say Be strong in the Lord, in the power of his might, Put on the whole armor of God ,that you may be able to stand against the wiles of the devil.

4. God doesn't reward people who are selfishness.

For where jealous and selfish ambition exists, there will be disorder and every vile practice. (James 3:16-17)

5. God doesn't reward people who are thankful to Him.

God give us gifts and blessings and He expects us to go back to him and give thanks and praise Him.

It doesn't matter what people say about you because all things are possible with God. All that really matters is what God says about you, and what you think and say about yourself (Luke 17:11).

6. God doesn't reward people who are complaining.

God HATES complaining so much. One of Israel's greatness sin, their most constant sin while in the wilderness. In fact, it was their complaining that made an 11-day trip last for forty years. (Number 16:2)

God has given us the POWER over the enemy, and by now you know that poverty is clearly one of the tools the enemy has used to keep us weak and ineffective for the Kingdom. So now, you have this wonderful truth (keys) about abundance that is not just an impossible dream. It is a reality that is happening to you. You are possessing a new prosperity mentality in Jesus name.

"A decision not to change is a decision to remain the same."

CHAPTER 8

How to tap into your breakthrough

Breakthrough is a place of breaking forth with sudden force. If you want to break into a new season, new birth, new beginnings, you must have the anointing of the Holy Spirit as I call it "FORCE." That work through our life to go forth, break off and destroy all obstacles that hinders progress in our life, and cause you not to advance beyond the limitations. He is the powerful God, all by Himself. He is a great God who prepares a way of conquest for us. He goes in front of us to make a clear path to victory. Listen, we need the supernatural intervention of God to break through impassable gates in order to enter into new territories and new places.

Revelation 3:8 says, I know your works. See, I have set before you an open door, and no one can shut it, for you have a little strength, have kept my word, and have not denied my name.

In the book of Daniel says "And He changes the times and the seasons; He removes kings and raises up kings, He gives wisdom to wise and knowledge to those who have understanding."

On that day, the LORD will end the bondage of his people. He will break the yoke of slavery and lift it from their shoulders (Isaiah 10:27).

God wants to bring each one of us into a breakthrough experience. He has provided us with a breaker anointing that will shake loose everything that holds us back, our business and families as one who is conquering and leading the conquerors.

Jesus Christ goes before us and crushes gates and chains in our way in order to lead His people into an open area of fulfillment. He breaks people out of prison houses to give them their destined heritage. There is no obstacle too high or too low hard for Him to destroy.

What is your yoke? Is it a financial yoke? That yoke can be broken. God gave a financial plan over seven hundred years and it has not changed. Abraham at that time paid tithes, Jacob was a tither and God prospered both of them. The principle of God is, "Give, and it shall be given unto you" (Luke 6:38). Don't wait until God first give to you, He said from His word, give and it shall be given back to you in return. When you have taken God as your number one priority or as your partner, obey Him and let Him know you are expecting a good return. The bible tells us about how Elijah was fed by the birds during a famine.

Then, the Lord told Elijah, Arise, get thee to Zarephath… I have commanded a widow woman there to sustain thee (I Kings 17:9). God was providing that widow a chance to give to Him that He might give to her. He would ask her to give all and if she did, great blessings were to follow. Elijah said to her, "Bring me, please, a piece of bread."

As surely as the Lord your God lives," she replied, "I don't have any bread only a handful of flour in a jar and a little olive oil in a jug. I am gathering a few sticks to take home and make a meal for myself and my son that we may eat it and die." When you're down that low, you may just as well give your last bread to God because you'll soon meet Him. God doesn't want you to wait until you are out of debt before you pay your tithes and love offerings. God said if you fail in your tithes and offerings that you have robbed Him of His entitlements. Bring the whole tithe into the storehouse, that there may be food in my house. Test me in this, "says the Lord Almighty, and see if I will not throw open the floodgates of heaven and pour out so much blessing that there will not be room enough to store it" (Malachi 3:10).

Sometimes, we forget that it was from nothing that God created the whole universe. He can perform a miracle for you out of absolutely nothing! All He wants is for you to get ready so He can use you; you are the channel He must work through.

The Lord promised that when things become worse than you could bear, He would provide a way of escape. If there is none, then you can bear a little more. He will give you grace and help for your situation.

God will supply your needs if you look to Him for help and are obedient. Simon needed money to pay taxes, and Jesus told him go down to the sea. Cast a hook, and take up the fish that first cometh up, and when thou hast opened his mouth, thou shalt find a piece of money, take that and give unto them for me and thee (Matthew 17:27).

What fantastic ways the Lord uses to provide for His people! Get ready for God's miracle. Get ready for God to move for you, prepare for your yoke to be broken, no matter the situation looks like! In Jesus name.

Perhaps, your yoke is one of your sickness. Others have been healed by God, definitely you too can! We have not come to the perfection in God's Word, His love and His anointing that we can understand all. We do not know why it is so easy for some to receive a miracle from God and so hard for some others. But we do know that we must get ready, do all we know and then wait upon God for the miracle. The Bible says that WITH HIS STRIPES WE ARE HEALED!

Perhaps, your yoke is a spiritual one. You just cannot seem to pray right to save your life because you don't believe your prayers will really be answered. You are unable to get the words straightened out in your mind or to think clearly. In fact, half of the time you're not even sure you are saved. The devil comes in on that channel of insecurity and just makes hash out of you. Your mind is tormented, worried about something all the time. A nervous, uneasy burden presses down on you and you don't know why. If you don't know what your burden is all about, go in before God and let the Holy Spirit unwrap the burden. God does not expect you to carry burdens you cannot identify.

Keep your mind on the greatness of God and the marvelous promises He has given you. With Jesus, with the anointing of God, every day is yours and things will be made wonderful. The anointing of God breaks the yoke. Come out of bed in the morning using that anointing and believe that you must have it each day that passes by. Take time to liberate the inside of you. Arise saying, "Thank God, I have Jesus. I'm going to be an overcomer today, because you walk with me LORD.

The Word brings Heaven within your reach and abundant life to you. Jesus said, I came that they might have life, and that they might have it more abundantly (John 10:10).

God can free us from any situations, but you have to be willing to abide in Him and obey His voice or live the life that glorifies Him.

- **Four things you need to know that can help to obtain your breakthrough**

1. You can attain a breakthrough by abiding in Him. Abiding in Him is to stay in the word of God daily. There must be a steady and stable routine of bible reading and application. Now, when applying the word of God it all boils down to the abiding, if you don't read there's nothing to apply. Those who abide in the Lord can live without the fear of what the devil will do. The bible says,

Jesus never did anything unless the Father told Him to do. That means He was in constant communication with the Father. We can be there if we are daily in the word of God because Father (God) speaks through His Word. Keep in mind that even though God promised your healing, protection or blessings, it doesn't guarantee that the devil will leave you alone. The hope we have is believing that God will give us a way of escape every time the devil rears his ugly head at us.

2. You can attain a breakthrough by focusing on Jesus and letting the Spirit of the Lord that is within you lead you through. The Deuteronomy 4:29 says, "But from there you will seek the Lord your God, and you will find Him if you seek Him with all your heart and with all your soul."

3. You can attain a breakthrough by faith. The 1 Kings 17:16 says, That woman made a bread or Elijah first. It took great faith, for not only her life, but also the life of her son was at stake. To think that she would give that last handful of meal to the man of God rather than her own son is hard for many to imagine. When she went back to that jar of flour, it was filled and running over, and the jug oil filled up too. And the barrel of meal wasted not, neither did the jug of oil fail, according to the word of the Lord, which He spoke through Elijah. It wasn't magic or luck a rather it came about through faith in God. The widow's yoke had been broken through faith in the anointing of God. She gave her last to God and found that she could never out-give God. The anointing in Elijah's life helped bring about deliverance for that

woman. Miracle power worked massively in Elijah's life and that miracle power broke the bondage. God can work a miracle for your needs no matter the form they come in, be it physical, mental, spiritual or financial.

4. You can attain a breakthrough by obedience. Obedience always brings blessings. The Deuteronomy 28:1-14, If you fully obey the Lord your God and carefully follow all his commands I give you today, the Lord your God will set you high above all the nations on earth. All these blessings will come on you and accompany you if you obey the Lord your God. You will be blessed in the city and be blessed in the country. The fruit of your womb will be blessed, and the crops of your land and that of your young livestock—the calves of your herds and the lambs of your flocks. Your basket and your kneading trough will be blessed. You will be blessed when you come in and blessed when you go out. The Lord will grant that the enemies who rise up against you will be defeated before you. They will come at you from one direction but flee from you in seven. The Lord will send a blessing on your barns and on everything you lay your hands on. The Lord your God will bless you in the land He is giving you. The Lord will establish you as His holy people, just as He promised you on oath, if only you keep the commands of the Lord your God and walk in obedience with Him. Then all the people on earth will see that you are called by the name of the Lord, and they will fear you. The Lord will grant you abundant prosperity in the fruit of your womb, the young of

your livestock and the crops of your ground in the land He swore to your ancestors to give you. The Lord will open the Heavens, the storehouse of His bounty to send rain on your lands in season and to bless all the work of your hands. You will lend to many nations but will borrow from none. The Lord will make you the head and not the tail. If you pay attention to the commands of the Lord your God that I give you this day and carefully follow them, you will always be at the top, never at the bottom. Do not turn aside from any of the commands I give you today, either to the right or to the left following other gods and serving them.

The Bible also speaks about the Curses for Disobedience from the same book of Deuteronomy 28:15-68,

"If you do not obey the Lord your God and do not carefully follow all his commands and decrees I am giving you today, all these curses will come on you and overtake you: You will be cursed in the city and cursed in the country. Your basket and your kneading trough will be cursed. The fruit of your womb will be cursed, and the crops of your land, and the calves of your herds and the lambs of your flocks. You will be cursed when you come in and cursed when you go out. The Lord will send on you curses, confusion and rebuke in everything you put your hand to, until you are destroyed and come to sudden ruin because of the evil you have done in forsaking him.[a] The Lord will plague you with diseases until he has destroyed you from the land you are entering to possess. The Lord will strike you with wasting disease, with fever and inflammation, with scorching heat and drought, with blight and mildew, which will plague you until you perish. The sky over your head will be bronze, the ground beneath you iron. The Lord will turn the rain of your country into dust and powder; it will come down from the skies until you are destroyed. The Lord will cause you to be defeated before your enemies. You will come at them from one direction but flee from them in seven, and you will become a thing of horror to all the kingdoms on earth. Your carcasses will be food for all the birds and the wild animals, and there will be no one to frighten them away. The Lord will afflict you with the boils of Egypt and with tumors, festering sores and the itch, from which you cannot be cured. The Lord will afflict you with madness, blindness and confusion of mind. At midday you will grope about like a blind person in the dark. You will be unsuccessful in everything you do; day after day you will be oppressed and robbed, with no one to rescue you. You will be pledged to be married to a woman, but another will take her and rape her. You will build a house, but you will not live in it. You will plant a vineyard, but you will not even begin to enjoy its fruit. Your ox will be slaughtered before your eyes, but you will eat none of it. Your donkey will be forcibly taken from you and will not be returned. Your sheep will be given to your enemies, and no one will rescue them. Your sons and daughters will be given to another nation, and you will wear out your eyes watching for them day after day, powerless to lift a hand. A people that you do not know will eat what your land and labor produce, and you will have nothing but cruel oppression all your days. The sights you see will drive you mad. The Lord will afflict your knees and legs with painful boils that cannot be cured, spreading from the soles of your feet to the top of your head. The Lord will drive you and the king you set over you to a nation unknown to you or your ancestors. There you will worship other gods, gods of wood and stone. You will become a thing of horror, a byword and an object of ridicule among all the peoples where the Lord will drive you. You will sow much seed in the field but you will harvest little, because locusts will devour it. You will plant vineyards and cultivate them but you will not drink the wine or gather the grapes, because worms will eat them. You will have olive trees throughout your country but you will not use the oil, because the olives will drop off. You will have sons and daughters but you will not keep them, because they will go into captivity. Swarms of locusts will take over all your trees and the crops of your land. The foreigners who reside among you will rise above you higher and higher, but you will sink lower and lower. They will lend to you, but you will not lend to them. They will be the head, but you will be the tail. All these curses will come on you. They will pursue you and overtake you until you are destroyed, because you did not obey the Lord your God and observe the commands and decrees he gave you. They will be a sign and a wonder to you and your descendants forever. Because you did not serve the Lord your God joyfully and gladly in the time of prosperity, therefore in hunger and thirst, in nakedness and dire poverty, you will serve the enemies the Lord sends against you. He will put an iron yoke on your neck until he has destroyed you. The Lord will bring a nation against you from far away, from the ends of the earth, like an eagle swooping down, a nation whose language you will not understand, a fierce-looking nation without respect for the old or pity for the young. They will devour the young of your livestock and the crops of your land until you are destroyed. They will leave you no grain, new wine or olive oil, nor any calves of your herds or lambs of your flocks until you are ruined. They will lay siege to all the cities throughout your land until the high fortified walls in which you trust fall down. They will besiege all the cities throughout the land the Lord your God is giving you. Because of the suffering your enemy will inflict on you during the siege, you will eat the fruit of the womb, the flesh of the sons and daughters the Lord your God has given you. Even the most gentle and sensitive man among you will have no compassion on his own brother or the wife he loves or his surviving children, and he will not give to one of them any of the flesh of his children that he is eating. It will be all he has left because of the suffering your enemy will inflict on you during the siege of all your cities. The most gentle and sensitive woman among you—so sensitive and gentle that she would not venture to touch the ground with the sole of her foot—will begrudge the husband she loves and her own son or daughter the afterbirth from her womb and the children she bears. For in her dire need she intends to eat them secretly because of the suffering your enemy will inflict on you during the siege of your cities. If you do not carefully follow all the words of this law, which are written in this book, and do not revere this glorious and awesome name—the Lord your God— the Lord will send fearful plagues on you and your descendants, harsh and prolonged disasters, and severe and lingering illnesses. He will bring on you all the diseases of Egypt that you dreaded, and they will cling to you. The Lord will also bring on you every kind of sickness and disaster not recorded in this Book of the Law, until you are destroyed. You who were as numerous as the stars in the sky will be left but few in number, because you did not obey the Lord your God. Just as it pleased the Lord to make you prosper and increase in number, so it will please him to ruin and destroy you. You will be uprooted from the land you are entering to possess. Then the Lord will scatter you among all nations, from one end of the earth to the other. There you will worship other gods—gods of wood and stone, which neither you nor your ancestors have known. Among those nations you will find no repose, no resting place for the sole of your foot. There the Lord will give you an anxious mind, eyes weary with longing, and a despairing heart. You will live in constant suspense, filled with dread both night and day, never sure of your life. In the morning you will say, "If only it were evening!" and in the evening, "If only it were morning!"—because of the terror that will fill your hearts and the sights that your eyes will see. The Lord will send you back in ships to Egypt on a journey I said you should never make again. There you will offer yourselves for sale to your enemies as male and female slaves, but no one will buy you."

God intended that we become winners. He did not plan for us to be wallowing in defeat in all our endeavors rather He gave us dominion over the earth and everything and breathed there. It doesn't matter how much you feel like a loser, it doesn't matter how much times you have failed in the past. If you believe Jesus is the breaker anointing and yoke destroyer, you will not be defeated anymore.

It is important to note that Jesus came to set the captives free and He accomplished that at the Calvary tree on His mission and what He came to do. Now, if we want to live in that freedom, you definitely CAN.

"God will supply your needs if you look to Him and be obedient."

CHAPTER 9

What are you doing to keep the fire of God burning inside you?

As believers in Jesus Christ, we are called upon to offer our bodies as "living sacrifices" (Romans 12:1), engulfed by the divine gift which is the inextinguishable fire of the Holy Spirit. At the very beginning of the New Testament, we saw so many times that the Holy Spirit is associated with fire. John the Baptist predicts that Jesus will be the One to "baptize you with the Holy Spirit and with fire."

The book of Matthew 3:11 says, When the Holy Spirit began His ministry of indwelling the early church, He chose to appear as "tongues of fire" resting on each of the believers. The Spirit is like a fire and some of His works is to bring God's presence, God's passion, and God's purity to us. The Holy Spirit is the presence of God as He indwells in the heart of a believer.

For that reason, all believers have the power of the Holy Spirit that dwell in us. However, that power will not work until we put it to work. It needs to be activated.

It's now the time to step out on our own and welcome the Holy Spirit to take over, so He can bring fire into our life.

Luke 24:32 says, And they said one to another, Did not our heart burn within us, while he talked with us by the way, and while he opened to us the scripture. The Holy Spirit creates the passion of God in our hearts and it described their hearts as "burning within us."

You can live a life of extraordinary, supernatural power! The secret is very simple. God's power is obtained through a lifestyle of intimacy with Him. And the only way to have an intimacy with God is by reading His word so as acquire those extraordinary powers. It's that simple!

Psalms 33:4 says, The Word of the Lord is right and true"

Also Proverbs 30:5 says "Every word of God proves true; he is a shield to those who take refuge in him." Trust in the word of God and know that it is altogether true. That means that everything written in the Bible is true. It is true about salvation and the Holy Spirit as we have been following all along. Let the word of God strengthen, restore you, and support you as you seek Him in all areas of your life.

Colossians 1:11 says; strengthened with all power, according to His glorious might, for the attaining of all steadfastness and patience; joyously.

Take a look at your life now. If you no longer have the fire in your burning, there is a big chance that you will easily give up when trials and obstacles come your way.

So, here are few things that you can do to keep your fire lit and strong at all time with an armor of faith.

1. Keep a strong relationship with Jesus.

He is the CENTER of our life and through Him we will get to see His Father who is God. So, spend time alone with God in prayer regularly. Remember, it's during prayer that God's Spirit touches your spirit.

2. Walk in the Holy Spirit.

No matter how hard you may try, you can't become the person God wants you to be through your own efforts. The only way to do so is to live with God's Spirit flowing through you like a river of living water that makes you and those you relate with to flourish.

3. Kill your flesh.

Stop chasing after the versions of yourself that will only interfere with you becoming the person God intends you to be. In other words, I meant to say stop pleasing people rather please God alone.

4. Pray in the Holy Ghost.

When you pray, the Spirit makes it perfect, builds you up, renew you, restore and strengthen your spirit

5. Commit to follow God where He leads.

Decide to surrender every part of your life to God every day and see His light shine all over you.

6. Don't let your desire to drive you.

Say "Lord I give you my desire" and let him replace your desire with His own.

7. Deal with sin wisely.

Talk with God regularly about your problems and desires. Be honest about when you're facing temptation, and ask God to help you overcome it. Because sin is a fire-quencher. The bible says, His kindness leads us to repentance and God draws nearer to us especially to the humble, repentant heart.

8. Deal with challenges well.

Trust God to bring something good out of even the most challenging situations you go through. God will give you wisdom and a sense of compassion in the process to help you.

9. Learn to Trust God.

Choose to trust God even when you feel afraid. As you move forward in trust, God's perfect love will flow through you and cast out your fears. (Proverbs 3:5-6), "Trust in the Lord with all your heart, and lean not on your own understanding; in all your ways acknowledge Him, and He will direct your paths."

10. Follow the guidance of the Holy Spirit.

The Holy Spirit guides us into God's will. Ps. 143:10: "Teach me to do Your will, for You are my God; Your Spirit is good. Lead me in the land of uprightness."

God is pouring out His Holy Spirit (Fire). "But this is what was spoken by the prophet Joel: 'And it shall come to pass in the last days, says God, That I will pour out of My Spirit on all flesh; Your sons and your daughters shall prophesy, Your young men shall see visions, Your old men shall dream dreams. And on My menservants and on My maidservants I will pour out My Spirit in those days; And they shall prophesy. (Acts 2:16-18)

Ask God to make you a HOUSE of prayer day and night and not to let the fire in your alter to burn out. Ask Him to sustain you as you walk in His marvelous light daily.

Tell God you want to seek His face.

"You can live a life of extraordinary, supernatural power! The secret is very simple. Have a good relationship with God."

"Let the word of Christ dwell in you richly in all wisdom, teaching and admonishing one another with psalms, hymns and spiritual songs, singing with grace in your hearts to God."

Chapter 10

Protecting and Monitoring your Fire

Sometimes, our fire (Holy Spirit) can be tempted or crashed when difficult things happen if only we give in to them. So, you have to know how to stay filled and know how to prevent your fire from going off or crashed.

We have the world system that constantly tempts and at times even persecutes us. We have an enemy, the devil seeking to distract us away from God. Because of all these realities, there is a need to protect our fire.

Yes! You're filled with the fire of the Holy Ghost now. But what am trying to say to you is, you have to know how to protect your FIRE as a believer and if for any reason the presence of the Holy Spirit (fire) tries to leave you, I believe at this point you already know what to do to make the fire continue to burn inside of you and if the fire is dead then you need to know how to start the fire again. Right?

Woman of Fire

Ok, First of all, caring for our spiritual fire can take a little conscious planning and intentionality because there are strategies that can keep you going throughout .Here are some of my own techniques I use. And through them, I achieved great victories in my life. So if it works for me, I believe it will work for you too.

Let's start,

The Holy Spirit gave me the revelation of using physical fire as an example to define how the spiritual fire works for easy understanding.

Think about the physical fire and the process it takes to start a fire.

First, you have to make sure you're stocked with good fuel supplies (materials) like, woods, dry leaves, fluff, newspaper, cotton swabs ,toilet paper and cattail, in order to start the dwindle or keeping the one you have from going out. Right?

Second, put your materials together like dry leaves, or newspaper, then add kindling, and finally wood to keep your fire from going out. Then you'll have to repeat the process throughout the entire time to keep the fire burning. But as you repeating the process, you have to make sure your putting good dry woods to sustain the fire.

Remember, all the wood you use to build your fire should be completely dry. If there's any moisture left in the wood, it will be harder to keep a fire going. Instead, you might end up with a pile of smoking wood.

Why dry firewood? "Because it will catch quickly and sustain a nice burn."

These are same methods I use to monitor and protect my "Spiritual Fire."

Our "spiritual fire" can be ignited as easily as a modern furnace, but I will start by saying this; God wants us to protect our fire. We cannot sit back and say, "God will protect me" if we have not done the things we ought to be doing.

From the book of Roman 8:9 says, But when the Spirit of Christ empowers your life, you are not dominated by the flesh but by the Spirit. And If your not joined to the Spirit of the Anointed one, you are not of him.

Simply is to say, "If anyone doesn't have the Spirit of Christ, he doesn't belong to Christ." Let us learn and motivate one another on how to keep the Holy Spirit with us. The Holy Spirit will never leave or forsake a true believer.

Ephesians 1:13-14"And you also were included in Christ when you heard the message of truth, the gospel of your salvation. When you believed, you were marked in him with a SEAL, the promised Holy Spirit, who is a deposit guaranteeing our inheritance until the redemption of those who are God's possession to the praise of His glory."

The Holy Spirit is a gift that Jesus promised to leave with us when you read from John 14:16, "And I will ask the Father, and he will give you another advocate to help you and be with you forever."

But the only thing that can make Holy Spirit to depart from us is SIN .You can see another view of the Holy Spirit from the book of

1 Samuel 16:14, the Holy Spirit indwelt King Saul, but then departed from him. Instead the Spirit came upon David.

But see this, After David adultery with Bathsheba, He feared that the Holy Spirit would be taken from him (Psalm 51:11).

1. Sin

Sin Always has consequences in our relationship with God. While our relationship with God is secure in Christ, unconfessed sin in our lives can hinder our fellowship with God and effectively quench the Holy Spirit's working in our lives. That is why it is so important to confess our sins because God is "faithful and just and will forgive us our sins and purify us from all sinful traces."

2. New believer

If you are a new believer, ask the Lord to deliver you from manipulators of the Bible by allowing the Spirit to directly teach you God's truth from the scriptures. Find a church or a group of believers who are on fire for Jesus.

John 16:13 says,

"But when he, the Spirit of truth, comes, he will guide you into all the truth. He will not speak on his own; he will speak only what he hears, and he will tell you what is yet to come." The Holy Spirit will give you wisdom to see through the manipulative tricks of ambitious leaders.

3. Be effective in doing things of God.

In ancient Israel, the priests were instructed not to let the fire on the altar go out (Lev. 6:9, 12-13). This required a lot of work, not the least of which was collecting firewood in a land not known for its dense forests.

Some scholars see the fire on the altar as a symbol for the flame of our devotion with the Lord. Spiritual passion is not something to be treated lightly or taken for granted. It will grow cold if we fail to keep it supplied with fuel. We need to be steadfast to keep the light on.

The apostle Paul addressed the subject of spiritual fervor in his letter to the Romans (12:1-2, 11). To keep the fire of our devotion burning strong, we must continue the hard work of stocking our fuel supply with hope, patience, steadfast prayer, generosity, hospitality, and humility.

4. Control your mind

Control what goes to your brain. If you listen to the bad stuffs and negative conversations, that's exactly who you will become. So, try to develop a habit of listening to worship music, download sermons or an audio version Bible to your phone or tablet. The more you listen to God's word, the more powerful and stronger your faith becomes. Apostle Paul says from the book of Romans 8:6; The mind governed by the flesh is death, but the mind governed by the Spirit is life and peace. Ask the Lord to protect your mind day and night. Let us not be conformed to this world, but be transformed by the renewing of our minds that we may prove what Your will is, that which is good, acceptable and perfect.

5. Utilize your free time wisely.

What if we read the Bible to our kids, spouses or to ourselves, play worship music while cooking dinner or go to bed marinating in faith-filled books on CD instead of plunking in front of the TV each night? Wouldn't we be closer to God at the end of the day?

We know that our struggle is not against flesh and blood, but against the rulers, against the powers, against the world forces of this darkness, against the spiritual forces of wickedness in the heavenly places. So, let us dress ourselves in God's armor so that we can stand firm in Him.

6. Let the car be your sanctuary.

The Scripture tells us we are the temple of the living God. Don't wait until you're in the church to praise and worship the Lord. Just turn your music on and give God praise while driving.

7. Get Scripture texts or tweets.

Go online and request for Scripture to be sent to your phone or email daily as texts or tweets. You will be amazed at how God will use these medium to speak to you daily.

8. Serve.

You might be surprised at the benefits in service. Teaching your child's Sunday school class, reading kids the Bible or choosing a Christian nonprofit to do service hours or an internship will certainly ignite the flame of faith inside you. We must grow our faith, become sanctified and connected with Christ not when we are "getting" but when we are giving our lives away.

9. Walk in Spirit

Trust the Holy Spirit in you...He knows what's best for you and your soul. Our part is to pray, study God's Word, and learn to develop our own sensitivity and obedience to the Holy Spirit's lead.

Go ahead and apply them today. I promise you that your spiritual life will never be boring with Him in the lead.

> "O God, my heart is the altar
> And my love for you is the flame;
> I'll keep the fire burning for You, Lord,
> And I will rejoice in Your name."

"God let the FIRE in my altar never burn out."

CHAPTER 11

Importance of Fasting, Praying, Word of God & Faith in God.

Both the Old Testament and New Testament teaches the value of fasting, which is abstaining from food or drinks in order to focus solely on prayer and seeking God's will. Through many examples in the Bible of those who fasted, we can know that God grants supernatural revelation and wisdom through this practice. The Bible tells us that fasting will help us grow a more intimate relationship with Jesus and will open our eyes to what He wants to teach us.

Biblical fasting is a spiritual discipline which was encouraged by Jesus Himself, while He was on earth. When questioned as to why the Pharisees and the disciples of John the Baptist fasted while Jesus disciples did not, Jesus answered, "How can the guests of the bridegroom mourn while he is with them? The time will come when the bridegroom will be taken from them; then they will fast" (Matthew 9:15).

Do you know that fasting leads you to greater intimacy with the LORD?

Here are 23 spiritual benefits fast can bring to you.

1. Our spirit and soul experience joy because of fasting.
2. We are bringing ourselves in alignment with God.
3. We gain spiritual strength through fasting.
4. Our spirits are revived and refreshed.
5. We gain wisdom and guidance through fasting.
6. We develop a lifestyle of servant living.
7. We are able to discern the will of God through fasting and deep prayer.
8. Fasting opens the room for God to fill us with His Holy Spirit.
9. It cleans the soul by fasting and meditating.
10. We ignite Holy Spirit Fire as we fast and pray
11. Empowerment flows when we fast and pray.
12. We destroy spiritual opposition and satanic strongholds.
13. We get equipped to deal with the momentary trial we face on earth.
14. Desire God in a new way.
15. We become sensitive to God's voice.
16. Position ourselves for a breakthrough.
17. To kill idols.
18. A closer union with God.
19. To build our faith to God.
20. Focus deeper on God.

21. It brings genuine repentance.

22. To show obedience to the Lord.

23. We gain spiritual self-control.

Veronica Abisay

How do we pray to God?

Pray without season. What is your prayer life?

Paul says from the book of 1 Thessalonians 5:17 that we are to pray without ceasing. Those are just three simple words, and yet they carry a life changing message if we actually apply them.

What does it mean to "pray without ceasing?" Well, this verse focuses on our heart attitude. It does not mean that we spend the entire day on our knees praying without engaging in any other activity. If we did that, we would not be able to keep a job, pay our bills or take our kids to school.

The directive to "pray without ceasing" means that we are to be ever present with God throughout the entire day. We are continually interacting with Him in prayer as we move from task to task. When we come across challenges, we ask for His assistance, when experience blessings, we thank Him for His favor, when we face temptations, we should take temptations before God and ask for His help. When you meet someone who does not know Jesus Christ, you pray for God to use you as His vessel to draw that person closer to Himself.

For believers, prayer should be like breathing. When we are born into the family of God, we enter into a spiritual atmosphere where God's presence and grace applies pressure on our lives. The pressure to love Him and do His will.

Prayer is essentially putting your request, concern, or issue before the Lord, and trusting Him to answer them adequately. Matthew 18:3 says "Truly I tell you, unless you change and become like little children, you will never enter the kingdom of heaven." Therefore, we need to pray with the heart of little children, which is simple, reverent, specific, and trusting.

Also Matthew 26:40-41 says, "Then [Jesus] came to the disciples and found them sleeping, and said to Peter, "What! Could you not watch with Me one hour? Watch and pray, lest you enter into temptation. The spirit indeed is willing, but the flesh is weak."

Mark 13:32-37 (Jesus talking about His second coming)"But of that day and hour no one knows, not even the angels in heaven, nor the Son, but only the Father. Take heed, watch and pray; for you do not know when the time is. It is like a man going to a far country, who left his house and gave authority to his servants, and to each his work, and commanded the doorkeeper to watch. Watch therefore, for you do not know when the master of the house is coming in the evening, at midnight, at the crowing of the rooster, or in the morning lest, coming suddenly, he find you sleeping. And what I say to you, I say to all: Watch!"

As you can see from the scriptures above, Jesus was praying all the time and making sure He is in a good communication with His Father. Jesus is our role model and mentor.

He taught His disciples how to pray.

He knew that prayer is the only way that can make you have "a close discussion" with God. The same teachings applies to us, because as believers of Jesus Christ, we must adopt the lifestyle of our Lord Jesus. He want us to have a prayer-lifestyle to maintain our relationship with. God loves us!

Moses prayed to God almost constantly on behalf of the Israelites for God's mercy and graciousness in dealing with their sins. Abraham prayed persistently for his relative Lot, who lived in Sodom that God would spare Him.

Asa cried out to the Lord. From the book of 2 Chronicles 14:11 says, "Then Asa called to the LORD his God and said, "LORD, there is no one like you to help the powerless against the mighty. Help us, LORD our God, for we."

Prophet Jeremiah prayed for God's guidance and protection of the Israelites. Jeremiah 10:23-24,

David prayed for the peace of Jerusalem in Psalm 122:6.

Matthew 6; 9-13

Verse 9: Jesus says we should give honor to God and His name. Verse 10: We are to pray for His Kingdom to come, and for His will to be done, that there would be a heavenly or godly presence here on earth. Verse 11: We are to pray for daily provision. Verse 12: We are to pray and ask for forgiveness for our sins, and for others who have wronged us. Verse 13: We are to pray and ask God to keep us from being tempted, and to deliver us from Satan and his power.

While we await the return of the bridegroom, our Lord Jesus Christ, fasting exemplifies our attitude of spiritual hunger and thirst, the promise is that we will be satisfied. "Blessed are those who hunger and thirst for righteousness, for they will be filled" (Matthew 5:6).

Also,2 Chronicles 7:14 says; If my people, who are called by my name, will humble themselves and pray and seek my face and turn from their wicked ways, then I will hear from heaven and will forgive their sin and will heal their land.

Fasting and prayer has taught me many things. It has made me stronger in my faith and I have learned that sometimes we just have to wait on the Lord and keep fasting and praying, trusting and believing that He will grant all our heart desires and request we bring to Him.

"Rejoice always, pray without ceasing, give thanks in all circumstances, for this is the will of God in Christ Jesus for you."

Veronica Abisay

Word of God

Why is the word of God so important to the believer?

The word of God is essential to believers because is divinely inspired by the Holy Spirit. The Apostle Paul wrote from the book of Timothy 3:16

"All scripture is God breathed and useful for teaching, rebuking, correcting, and training in righteousness, so that the man of God may be thoroughly equipped for every good work."

Hebrews 4:12 says, For the word of God is alive and active. Sharper than any double-edged sword, it penetrates even to dividing soul and spirit, joints and narrow, it judges the thoughts and attitudes of the hearts.

More reasons why the word of God is so important;

- Nourishing -Matthew 4:4, "man shall not live on bread, but on every word that proceeds out through the mouth of God." That means we get healthy nutrients by reading the word of God.
- Enlightening-Genesis 1:3, "God said let it be light. It means the word of God bring light into our inner being.
- Quenching your thirst-Isaiah 55:10-11"For just as the rain comes down and the snow from heaven and doesn't return there, until it waters the earth and makes it bear and sprout forth, so will my word be which goes forth from my mouth, it will not return to

me vainly, but will accomplish what I delight in, and will prosper in the matter to which to which I have sent it." By this word, the Bible indicates that God sent His word to water His people to accomplish His purpose in them.

- Strengthen-1 John 2:14 says, I have written to you, young men because you are strong and the word of God abide in you and you have overcome the evil one. It means the word of God makes us strong in our spirit and also in our soul.

- Cleaning-Ephesians 5:26-27, "That He {Christ} mighty sanctify her {the church}, cleansing her by the washing of the water in the word, that He might present the church to Himself glorious, not having spot or wrinkle or any such things, but that she should be holy and without blemish"-It means that the word of God is water that cleans all our sins and doubts.

- Building-Romans 12:4-5, "In the human body, there are many parts and organs, each with a unique function. And so it is with the body of Christ. For though, we are many, we've all been mingled into one body in Christ" This means that we are all vitally joined to one another, and also with each other contributing to the other.

- Empower-The word of God is powerful. You can only be empowered when you believe and apply it to your life. Joshua 1:9 says, "Have I not commanded you? Be strong and courageous. Do not be afraid; do not be discouraged, for the Lord your God will be with you wherever you go."

- Motivate-You will never go wrong using the Scripture to motivate yourself. God's Word is powerful by itself and it effectually works in the hearts of men too. Proverbs 3:5 says, "Trust in the Lord with all your heart, and do not lean on your own understanding."

When we let the word of God dwell in us, it will cause us to grow up into Christ, who is the Head of the body, thereby joining us together with His other growing believers and causing us to be built together as His own.

"The more we let the word of God dwell in us, the more virtues we will have."

Woman of Fire

"Faith comes by hearing and hearing the word of God. Read the word of God today."

Faith in God

It requires trusting God and believing that He loves you and that He has the power to help you through no matter the obstacle. We must learn to trust God in any situation. God knows us, knows what we need and want to meet those needs on our behalf, but unfortunately, we think that we know better than Him. Jeremiah 1:5 says, "Before I formed you in the womb I knew you, and before you were born I consecrated you; I appointed you a prophet to the nations." Long before we were conceived, God already knew of us, and by faith He could see us being conceived, formed, and born into this world. This means there isn't an accident for you to be in this world, it was His divine purpose that you breathe today on earth. You are a masterpiece of His work. He has a special purpose for you to fulfill in this world.

Knowing that it was God who knew us, and formed us, and called us into life, He is the backbone of our existence. When everything else around us is not making sense, this truth can give us the grounding that we desperately need to go on. We are all looking for a sense of meaning and purpose in our lives.

Look at this scripture, Isaiah 46:10
"Declaring the end from the beginning and from ancient times things not yet done, saying, 'My counsel shall stand, and I will accomplish all my purpose."

I used to have a habit of trusting people, getting hurt and finding out I couldn't trust them anymore. Then, I went through the word of God and decided to learn how to trust Him. I began to realize more and more about God's faithfulness to me. Look at this scripture that opened my eyes and shifted my trust from trusting people to trusting God.

Proverbs 3:5-6; "Trust in the Lord with all your heart, and lean not on your own understanding; in all your ways acknowledge Him, and He shall direct your paths. It means we don't have to go through someone else to cry out for help. God is our Provider. He dwells in our heart and we can learn to trust Him with all our strength and know that He will answer to our prayers or requests in His own time.

One of my very favorite things about God is that He is always faithful. Whenever He makes a promise, He keeps it. From the book of Numbers 23:19 says - God is not a man, that He should lie, Nor a son of man, that He should repent; Has He said, and will He not do it? Or has He spoken, and will He not make it good?

Just know that God will not let you to be tempted beyond your own ability, but with the temptation coming toward you, He will also provide the way of escape that you may be safe.

There are so many scriptures in the Bible that talk about how faithful God is, below are passages from the Bible that refer to God's trustworthiness, and faithfulness

- 1 Corinthians 1:9 - "God, who has called you into fellowship with his Son Jesus Christ our Lord, is faithful."

- 1 Corinthians 10:13 - "No temptation has seized you except what is common to man. And God is faithful; he will not let you be tempted beyond what you can bear. But when you are tempted, he will also provide a way out so you can stand up under it."

- 2 Thessalonians 3:3 - "The Lord is faithful, and he will strengthen and protect you from the evil one."

- Deuteronomy 7:9 ,Know therefore that the Lord your God is God, the faithful God who keeps covenant and steadfast love with those who love him and keep his commandments, to a thousand generations,

- Psalm 37:3 "Trust in the Lord, and do good. Dwell in the land and feed on His faithfulness."

- Psalm 33:4 "For the Word of the Lord is upright, And all His work is done in faithfulness."

  God is faithful to His Word. This is why it's imperative we know and speak His Word. When we speak the Word of God, it goes forth in power and God must back it up with action.

"God is always faithful and dependable. He cannot lie and will never break a promise"

"Rejoice always, pray without ceasing, give thanks in all circumstances, for this is the will of God in Christ Jesus for you."

CHAPTER 12

JOURNALING QUESTIONS

Question #1. What experience do you have in your walk with God every day?

Have you had moments you sensed the divine presence that God was near or closely watching you as you meditate, or have you prayed for guidance and felt you received it immediately?

Questions #2. Ask yourself each day before going to bed what you have done to keep your spirit healthy?

In order for you to stay healthy spiritually, you better have a habit of assessing yourself before the end of day and if you see everything is ok, then you have to give God praise and if you see something going wrong or missing then, set goals that will make you to reach where you want to be.

Questions #3. What ways naturally helps you to experience God's presence?

Is it about having devotional with Him, sharing the word with others or serving in the community?

For example, volunteer to the schools or help the elderly people. There are so many things that you can do that is up to you to know what are, the things that you do you feel good doing and at the same time they bring God's glory quick and fast, I urge you then to do it. Do it with excellence and with all of your heart .You will start to some see amazing things happening to your life.

Question #4. How's your prayer life?

We all make time for what we value the most. Have you gotten into the habit of praying to God on a regular basis? Make it a habit.

Question #5. Am I still carrying things, and doing things on my own that Holy Spirit came to do for me?

Seek the help from the Holy Spirit by choosing to humble yourself and give Him a full control.

Question #6. Do you really know this incredible POWER that lives in you?

As believer, we have the power of the Holy Spirit inside us. However, that power will not work until we put it to work. That is the key of activating that power and putting it to work.

Question #7. Do you daily set time in your schedule for reading bible?

Spiritual discipline is very important, we are called to study it and allow it to influence our lives.

CONCLUSION

At the conclusion, I will say this;

What matters most to God isn't what you do, it's who you are that counts in His presence. So pursuing certain accomplishments in life isn't nearly as important as becoming the person God created you to be. Use your time and energy well in serving the Lord. Focus on living up to your potential, growing into the person you really want to be and be that person God has created you to be. Someone who's free to live with love, joy and abundant life.

Get creative, and speak words that will uplift, encourage, hearten, and bless other people. Do the right things, allow God to be the CENTER of your life and I promise that your life will not remain the same and your spirit will get stronger and stronger in Him. I hope what I shared with you will encourage you to go higher in Jesus name.

May the Lord bless you and protect you in all that you do. May the Lord smile on you and be gracious to you. May the Lord show you His favor and give you His peace. And if you have not received Jesus Christ as your Lord and personal Savior, then let's take care of that right now. Read the following prayer out loud and give your life to Jesus Christ, so that you may be declared righteous through Him when the world is judged:

Lord Jesus,

Thank you for giving me an opportunity to be saved. Forgive me for the life of sin I've led and lived, and the resistance I've given you in the past. I'm deeply sorry. Today is a new day, a new day in your light. Fill me with your Holy Spirit, guide me in how to live, be the master of my life. You are my Lord, now and forever.

In your name, Lord Jesus, I pray,

Amen.

"God loves you"

When He created you in His magnificence, He created a
MASTERPIECE.

ACKNOWLEDGMENTS

SPECIAL THANKS TO MY HUSBAND, JOSEPH, for all his support on this project. Thanks to my friend and Soul Sister, Dr. Maria Asher Baptiste. Also, thanks to my biological sister, Aika A. Swai for her prayers and words of encouragements.

ABOUT THE AUTHOR

Veronica Abisay is a Tanzanian. She was raised by her parents (Pastor Abisay Swai and Minister Nipael Swai, and is the first born of four children, two sisters and a brother. She was schooled in Dar es Salama, Tanzania, Africa before going to study in the United States. She is a Minister, Information Technology Expert, and Serial Entrepreneur.

Ministry

Veronica Abisay's into the ministry started at the tender age of 15, as she received the Lord Jesus Christ as her personal Savior. Growing up in a Christian home she learned to praise and worship God, how to teach, preach, pray and fast, creating a deep foundation of the word & a fear of God.

Her life is dedicated to living a life pleasing to Christ and encouraging other women to walk in their purpose. She is the founder and visionary of the "Women of Fire Movement" that holds women's conferences, seminars, and revivals around the globe. She is also the founder of F&B Empire where she teaches women and girls to embrace their natural beauty and promotes healthy living by providing them with her products and programs.

You may connect with Veronica here:
website:www.veronicaabisay.com
Facebook: Veronica Abisay
Instagram: Veronica Abisay